Letter from the Editors

There were some teething problems with the last issue of the magazine because we had to switch printers but we have ironed out the kinks in time for the Christmas Issue. The one thing we're excited about the most is the better quality the new printer offers - we think the magazine looks the best it's ever looked.

After this issue, we'll be entering our third year of publishing the Anglotopia Magazine and there have been many ups and downs but we are looking forward to planning ahead for the next few years. With Facebook decimating small publishers like us, the print magazine is a key part of our future and we're going to continue it as long as we have reader support.

A bit of housekeeping, if you subscribed to the magazine when we first launched in 2015 and renewed last year in time for Issue 5, then this is your last issue - so please be on the lookout for your renewal notice in your email box. Thank you for coming along with us on this journey.

Speaking of journey, we have two trips to the UK planned for 2018. First is over the New Years holiday, our favorite cottage in Dorset, the closest place we have to a home in England, is being sold and we're going for a final stay. Expect a big article about that next year. And then if everything falls into place, we will be setting off on a journey to drive from Land's End to John O'Groats from one end of the United Kingdom to the other in late summer 2018. We can't wait to share our journeys with you!

Cheers,
Jonathan & Jackie
Publishers
Anglotopia

Table of Contents

How They Lived: Birmingham Back to Backs.........2
Brit Book Corner..12
Song: All Through the Night....................................14
Cadbury...16
A Very British Christmas...20
Lost in the Pond: Losing British Politeness...........24
Christmas in Wartime...26
Walpole: The First PM..32
This English Life: Comforts of Home...................36
Boxing Day 101..39
Christmas Food...40
Great British Icons: Penguin Books......................42
Christmas Actually: British Christmas Films........46
Tragedy of Lady Jane Grey....................................50
A British Christmas Dinner....................................54
Hovis Bread...60
The Slang Page..64

About the Magazine

The Anglotopia Magazine is published quarterly by Anglotopia LLC, a USA registered Corporation. All contents copyrighted and may not be reproduced without permission.

Letters to the Editors may be addressed to:

Anglotopia LLC
1101 Cumberland Crossing #120
Valparaiso, IN 46383
USA

Photos: Cover: Red Phone Box and Postbox in the Snow. Back cover: Covent Garden at Christmas. Inside Back Cover:

Printed in PRC

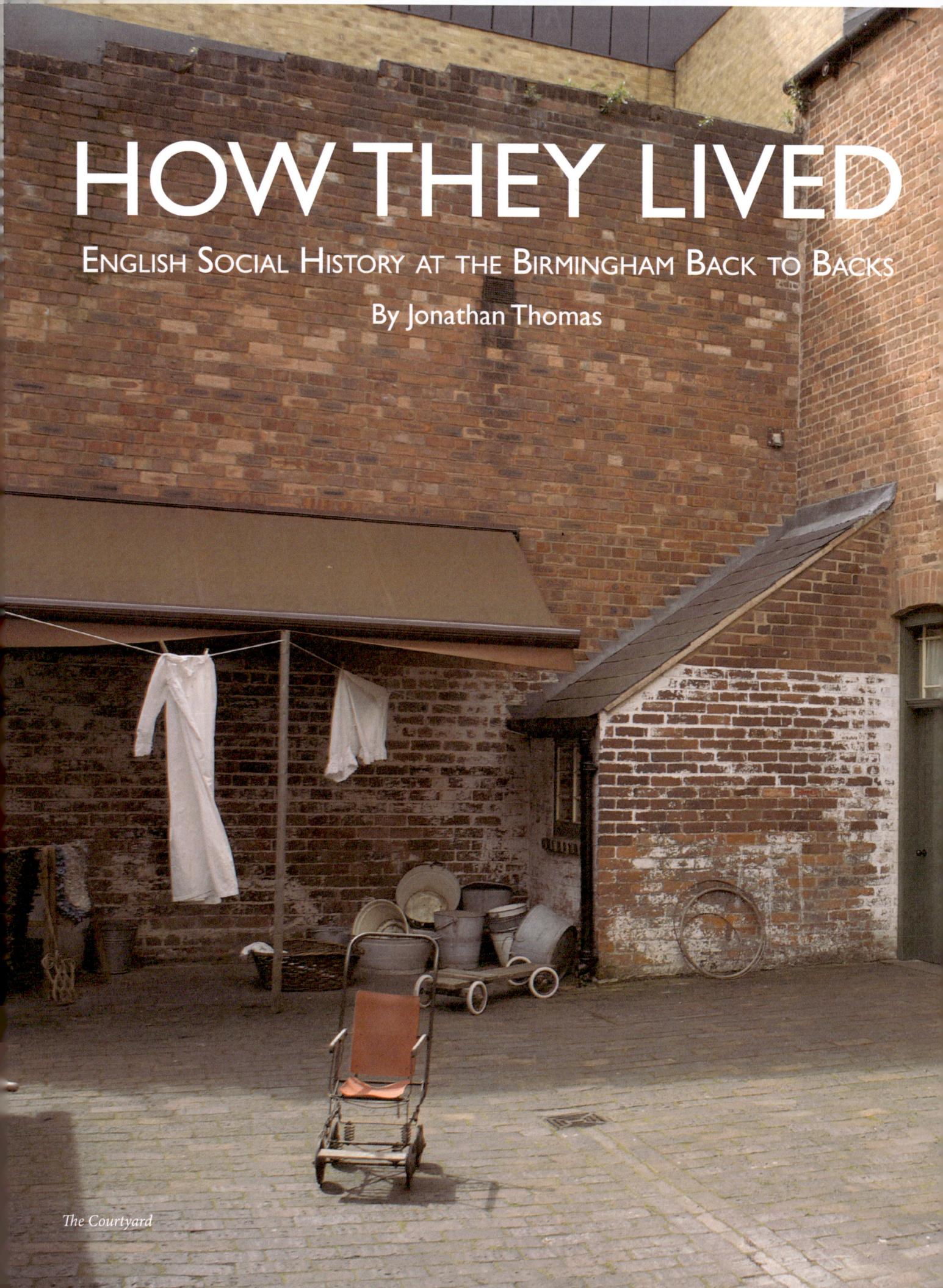

HOW THEY LIVED

English Social History at the Birmingham Back to Backs

By Jonathan Thomas

The Courtyard

The National Trust in England is mostly known as the organisation that preserves grand Stately Homes and the Countryside, but they have a secret. Well, it's not really a secret. But it's something that's not widely known; they also look after many important properties related to Britain's industrial and social heritage. One of the best is the Birmingham Back to Backs. This block of buildings in central Birmingham is a wonderfully preserved example of how people lived in the Victorian-era, at the height of industrialisation and mass migration to cities. The blocks located in Birmingham are the last Back to Backs in existence in Britain. The result is a time capsule of life long ago - warts and all that you can no longer see anywhere else. We had the opportunity to visit last year, and it was truly a remarkable experience.

With the start of the industrial revolution in 1820, Birmingham, then a city of about 50,000 people, became a thriving center of trade. This period saw many jobs open up and these needed to be filled. Those from rural areas and even other countries came seeking opportunity. Immigrants from Italy, Poland, Ireland, and Russia. Later, immigrants from far-flung Asian countries such as China came to make Birmingham their new home.

Birmingham saw a diverse community flourish as many came to work, but there was little housing to accommodate such a vast influx. In fact, by the end of the century, Birmingham was a city of more than 1 million people. Most people who migrated to this area came with very little means, financially and materially. The need for quick, cheap housing was urgent, and back to back court houses began being built.

The original builder, John Wilmore, bought land that contained a few workshops. The first evidence of residences being built came in 1802, with one larger house built in front and a smaller house in the back of the property. In the 1820s, more houses began to be built in a square formation that created a court in the middle, and in 1831, Court 15 was completed. Other landowners, seeing a financial advantage, followed suit, though none of their homes were quite as nice or as well built. Court 15 stood above the others in the fact that it was not only better built, but with its decorative window lintels and bay windows, it also had a nicer aesthetic. Eventually, a gas lamp was even installed in the courtyard to cut through the dark dreariness.

Far from the grand city homes found in wealthy London neighborhoods, back to back homes were small, overcrowded, and rather bleak. A court consisting of 11 houses often held as many as 66 people and were also eventually used for storage and workshops. Three toilets in the courtyard were the only facilities available and were to be shared by the entire court of homes as there were no such amenities inside. Tall chimneys jutted from each of the houses. As the only source of heat for warmth and cooking, they provided a steady stream of smoke that constantly left the courtyard cloudy and dark.

Owner landlords only had one concern while building these homes, and that was to make as much money as possible. Those who leased the land were allowed to decide for themselves how many homes they wanted to build on it. There were no laws or regulations governing the building work and no one to check to make sure that structures were well built. Therefore, workmanship was somewhat shoddy, and the homes were designed to pack in as many people as possible.

Each home contained two or three rooms for an entire family, and possibly even a lodger. The walls were only one brick deep which led to a number of issues. The thinness of the walls barely kept out weather elements. The homes were rather cold, and dampness seeped into the lower half of the walls and took up residence.

Such thin walls also lead to privacy issues. Not only could a family hear noise from their neighbors, the courtyard, and the street, their neighbors could hear them as well. It was nearly impossible to keep anything secret under these circumstances, and even private family matters such a fights or arguments became the business of everyone.

One of the first homes built (in Court 15) was inhabited by a Jewish family, Lawrence and Priscilla Levy and their four children, who migrated to Birmingham from London in 1851. Lawrence was a watchmaker by trade and living in the back to back houses there provided an easy access to work and supplies. Furthermore, there was an existing Jewish community in this area, complete with a synagogue and school for the children.

Their home is typical of many of the back to backs of that time period. The walls were decorated with stenciled patterns instead of wallpaper (there was a wallpaper tax, and only the wealthy could

afford it, so stenciling was the next best thing). Later on, those who could afford wallpaper were fortunate enough to have it as a minor insulating factor. Candles made from paraffin wax, or in the case of Jewish families like the Levys, candles made of lamb fat, were put in metal containers and used for lighting.

The Levy home had a comparatively large scullery which contained a lead sink. There was no indoor plumbing during this time, so water had to be collected from a nearby well using a bucket. Another bucket was kept under the sink to collect the waste water, which when full, had to be thrown out by hand. A cage containing eggs was hung from the ceiling in this room, keeping the food out of the reach of rats and mice. The scullery was used by Priscilla to prepare bread dough which was then taken down to the baker's shop for baking, to be later collected once it was once done. There was also a market in this area where not only fresh food could be bought, but also prepared and cooked meals—the mid-19th-century version of take-away.

Most back to back homes only had one bedroom, but the Levy home had two, making it the upper end of the back to back housing market. The Levys inherited a half tester bed, a piece of furniture which was not as warm or private as a 4-poster bed with a canopy, and certainly not as grand. But Its partial canopy over the head of the bead was enough to keep spiders and insects from falling onto sleeping faces. The bedroom also contained a storage trunk for clothes, and in the case of Priscilla, who was a dressmaker, also contained drapery. Like almost all other homes, theirs did not contain a closet or armoire as families did not have as many sets of clothing as people in modern times.

If a family had two bedrooms such as the Levys did, was typical for the female children to sleep in the same room as their parents, and the boys would sleep in the other bedroom. Most homes, however, only had one bedroom in which all family members would sleep. The parents would sleep on a bed with a feather mattress which had straw or horsehair underneath for warmth and support. It was customary practice to have babies sleep in a drawer until they were old enough to share a bed or cot with their siblings.

It was not unusual for families to take in a lodger (to bring in extra income and because it was difficult for single people to find accommodations) who also

Sitting Room in the Levy House

Shared bedroom, the screen was for lodger's privacy

shared the double bed, making for quite a crowd in the sleeping quarters. This made it all the more interesting when "nature called" in the middle of the night. A "guzzundah" (a toilet pan that went under the bed) was used, but with so many sleeping bodies around the room it could be difficult to find room to use it, and there was certainly no privacy in it. If the pan wasn't full after use, it went back under the bed. However, if it couldn't safely be used again, the liquid would be thrown out of the window. For solid waste, a bucket on the landing was used as a toilet, and it was the job of one unfortunate child to regularly empty this.

Each bedroom had a fireplace which was only used if someone was ill. The cost of wood and the heavy smoke which made it difficult to talk made it impractical for constant use. When cold, the family would take ash from the fire downstairs, and the embers were put in the hearth to take the chill out of the room. The cold (and often dampness) of the home, especially in freezing winter temperatures, made bed caps very important for conserving body heat.

Lawrence Levy most likely used part of the house for his workshop. All things in his shop would have been handmade, including tools such as his drills and saws. His 3-legged stool would have helped maintain his balance on the uneven floors. Because of heavy reliance on daylight, Lawrence worked long hours in the summer. The watchmaking business, also taken up by Lawrence's three sons, had become successful enough that the family was able to move to the more prestigious Jewelry Quarter in 1861.

Some families weren't as fortunate to have had a 2-bedroom home like the Levys. Smaller homes had a scullery one-third the size of the larger one and were used as a kitchen, storage, and laundry washroom. A small space such as this could be very challenging for larger families like the Oldfields who moved in around 1861. Given the high death rate of children during that time, and the complete lack of privacy, it was astonishing that Herbert and Ann Oldfield had no less than 10 children. Though large families had their joys and advantages, it no doubt put a strain on family finances and made feeding such a crowd quite the challenge.

Fresh fruits and vegetables were available in the neighborhood markets, but meat was very expensive, and most families could not afford it, at least not on a regular basis. Meals consisted mainly of stews with lentils to add bulk and protein. However, many families could afford to buy oysters. They were extremely inexpensive and plentiful, being brought by train from London on a daily basis. Due to the abundance and inexpensiveness of oysters, they were dubbed a poor man's meal. Other simple meals included a piece of bread with jam, cheese, or meat drippings when available. Fortunately, most families could also afford to buy ingredients to make sweets such as cakes and pastries. Large families like the Oldmans couldn't fit every family member around the table at the same time, so the family ate meals in relay fashion. Some children would be consigned to eating meals on the stairs.

Once a week a tin bath was brought out and put in front of the downstairs fire. Water had to be heated over the fire and then poured into the bath, something that took a long time with no modern conveniences. Due to this, families shared bath water, and the order in which each bathed reflected the hierarchy within the family. The youngest child would always be the last to bath, spurring the phrase "Don't throw the baby out with the bath water." Some parents would ladle water laundry tub into a smaller bin to wash young children, providing them with a somewhat cleaner source of bathwater. This practice went on all the way up until the 1940s.

In order to do laundry, children would be tasked with getting a fire lit and collecting water from the well. The laundry bin held 20 gallons of water which had to be brought in by heavy bucketfuls. Soap was expensive, so once the water was heated, a controlled amount of it put in the tub. A large stick was used to stir the laundry before it was transferred to a dolly to scrub out the stains and grime. The clothes were rinsed in cold water, hung out to dry, and then smoothed with heavy non-electric irons that were heated over hot coals. Care had to be taken that soot from the coals wasn't transferred from the iron to the clothes, dirtying them all over again. Clothes were then hung on lines in the court for drying. On the days when the weather outside was too damp for drying clothes, they were hung in the downstairs room in front of the fire. This was a bit tricky as clothes had to be close enough to the fire to dry, but not so close that they could be burned. The work was as arduous as it sounds.

Work outside the home was plentiful, but

could be difficult as well as dangerous for those that worked in the factories. Health and safety concerns in these workplaces were non-existent: Air quality often lead to chronic respiratory issues and machines had no safety guards to protect the workers. If an accident occurred, the employer took absolutely no responsibility for medical care or the protection of the worker's job. For example, if an employee lost a finger, more than likely they would end up losing their job along with their livelihood. There were no medical or disability benefits as in modern times.

However, Birmingham was called the City of 1,000 Trades, and those that had some sort of skill or training could find a certain amount of business success. Some of these trades, such as taxidermy, were what would be considered unusual now, but was a very popular trade in the Victorian era as stuffed animals were quite fashionable.

Then there was Herbert Oldman and his sons who practiced a specialty trade as glass toymakers, meaning they made the glass eyes for dolls and stuffed animals. Herbert may have even made glass eyes for human customers that had lost a real eye. It was claimed that his work was so realistic, not even someone's mate could tell the difference between the real eye and the manufactured eye. Like Lawrence Levy, it is likely that Herbert also used part of his home as his workshop as this would have been a far cheaper option than having to rent workspace.

As modernisation took place, the interior of the homes and their exterior courts saw many changes from the time of their first residents in 1820s and their last residents in 1966. Around the 1870s, improvements were slowly being made to houses where the landlord was sure that he could get enough rent to cover costs. Water taps were put into courtyards so residents could pump water instead of having to go down to the well with buckets.

Privies were installed in the courtyards to be shared by residents. There were no waste or water lines to these, and after each use, ash would have been put over the waste for some minimal coverage. When it was full, a neighbor would have to be kind enough to empty the waste into the same area as other household waste. The waste pile was then emptied once or twice a week and taken to a farm for compost. With 66 people using the privy, the smell could be overwhelming and germs prolific. Backhouses close to the privy were cheaper for this

The shared laundry rooms

reason. Going to the privy during the night had its dangers, and children always went to the courtyard in pairs. Before lamps were installed, the court was in complete darkness, and it was hard to know who could be there, including homeless people, mice, and rats. Conveniences such as toilet paper were also lacking, and a newspaper was used most of the time. Only during Christmas time, when gifts of oranges were wrapped in tissue paper, was there the "luxury" of using this for the toilet.

Gas lines began to be installed in order to light hurricane lamps that not only provided light to the courtyard but could be used in the winter to thaw water pipes. The homes never had hot water, but later gas boilers were installed.

Probably around the turn of the century, wires were run to give homes electricity, though this innovation was still in its infancy and there were no circuits as we have today. An adaptor needed to be used to plug anything in, and the electricity supply was mainly used for lighting. Overloading the system could cause a blowout or worse, set the home on fire. As time went on, early electric irons could fit into light sockets, though these irons had no controls. In later years, hand dusters were able to be replaced with vacuums.

Birmingham itself saw progress as time went on. Besides many successful trade shops, there were now places to eat and socialise. Municipal banks sprung up, and bank accounts were not just for the wealthy anymore. Patrons were given a locked money box though the bank kept the key. Money was put into the box and then taken to the bank where tellers would count it then put It into the patron's account. A well-established and high-end tailor shop moved into the area in the 1950s

The Mitchells were one family that lived through every change made to the back to backs. From whale oil lamps to electricity, three generations of Mitchells lived in Court 15. Beginning with Thomas and Ann in 1840, the family legacy of locksmithing and living in the court went on for 95 years. Their residence in the back to backs wasn't continuous though, as Thomas' son Benjamin became successful enough in the family's locksmith business to move out into the country. Like many who moved away and had a difficult time adjusting to a quieter life outside the noisy back to back courts, his son George moved back into Court 15 and continued the family business. Newer updates to the homes had given them more character, such as a posh brass bed. The homes still had no heating beyond the fireplaces, and many residents wore a coat to bed. Upgrading the bed, however, did nothing the control the infestation of bedbugs. Clever residents would build a fire until it was too hot to be in the room, and the bedbugs, also unable to stand the heat, would leave to find cool solace in a neighbor's home.

When later surveying was performed with a view to renovation, there was evidence that George Mitchell had done some renovation work on his own. No landlord came to check on what residents were doing, so he was free to change and build as he saw fit. Despite its problems, George lived and worked here until his death in 1935.

By 1966 no one was permitted to live in the deteriorating back to backs, though business was allowed to continue there. Once the most common working-class housing, the back to backs eventually became the rarest. By the 1990s, Court 15, in particular, was in terrible disrepair and rapidly deteriorating. There were holes in the roofs which made an inviting home of pigeons, and cats inhabited the cellars once used as bomb shelters during World War II.

The City of Hereford Archaeology Unit, along with the research team of the city council, agreed that the remarkable buildings found in Court 15 should be preserved. Renovation work was started, and after its completion in 2001, the Birmingham Conservation Trust took over its care to ensure its permanent survival. The houses opened to the public as a museum in 2004, now managed by the National Trust. For almost a century, millions of people lived in these slums, for good or ill. Now, this is all that remains to see a life that scarcely many of us can imagine. It's fantastic that such a huge piece of local and national British history, a history that still touches many families, will live on. If you can arrange a visit, it will be a very humbling and worthwhile experience.

Visiting Information

The Birmingham Back to Backs are open to the public through the National Trust, and all members (including Royal Oak Members) can get in for free. However, you MUST book ahead and arrange a tour by emailing them or calling. You can't just show up

Before the restoration.

and get a tour. Bookings fill up well in advance. The only way to see the houses is by guided tour. Email backtobacks@nationaltrust.org.uk to book tickets or call +441216667671. The Sweetshop is open daily and does not require advance booking. As the Back to Backs were built in the 19th century, they are NOT handicap accessible, and there are several narrow flights of stairs.

They're located in central Birmingham, so you can easily take the train right to Birmingham New Street station from London and walk to the Back to Backs which are only one-quarter mile away. We recommend sticking to public transport to get there, we drove because we were nearby, and Birmingham traffic was a nightmare of overcapacity and confusion.

Two of the properties have been converted into Holiday Lets by the National Trust and you can actually stay in them. They maintain the atmosphere of the old Back to Back but have all the modern amenities you would expect in a moder holiday let. You are central in Birmingham so there's plenty to see and do nearby. It will certainly be a special holiday to live amongst such interesting history.

BRIT BOOK CORNER

A Cottage in the Country by Jane Eastoe

A beautiful new book from Britain's National Trust which is a profile of all the quaint cottages in their collection. The book is filled with gorgeous pictures, lovely landscapes and tons of interesting history on each building. Perfect for reading with a cuppa. Pavilion $22.95

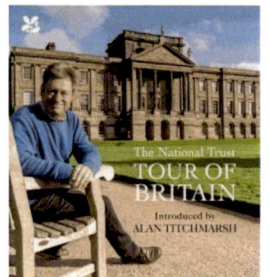

The National Trust Tour of Britain by Alan Titchmarsh

This is the kind of big glossy photographic book you'd see at a National Trust gift shop and immediately want to acquire. Alan Titchmarsh is a well-known British presenter and gardening enthusiast. He's done several great shows about Britain's heritage and natural landscape, so he's the perfect guide for a tour around Britain's heritage. This book doesn't just limit itself to National Trust owned properties, there's plenty they don't own. It's an excellent tour of Britain built and natural heritage and it will give you plenty of ideas for planning a trip to Britain. Tons of pretty pictures and useful information. You won't regret buying it. Pavilion $35.00

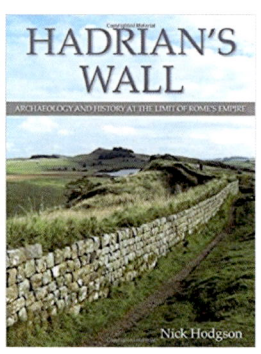

Hadrian's Wall by Nick Hodgson

One day I will walk the length of Hadrian's Wall in northern England (it's about 80 miles and takes a week, going from coast to coast). Until I'm able to, I will content myself with reading books like this. There are many books out there about Hadrian's Wall but this one is a new favorite of mine, it's engaging with a big focus on the archeological discoveries made along the walls. The book also has many illustrations to help understand the wall, how it was built and how it operated in reality. It's a treasure trove of information and is a must read for anyone considering doing the Hadrian's Wall Walk. Robert Hale $36.95

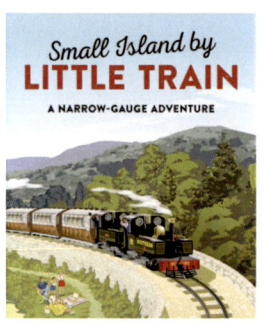

Small Island By Little Train by Chris Arnot

I'm a huge enthusiast for Britain's rails so I loved taking a look at this little book dedicated to Britain's narrow gauge railways. They're unique and quirky, often relics of industry that are now run by enthusiasts. Author Chris Arnot seeks to learn their stories and share them with us. From stalwart little locomotives of topographic necessity, to the maverick engines of one man's whimsy, Britain's narrow-gauge steam trains run on tracks a world apart from its regimented mainlines. Filled with pictures, maps and great stories, this is a fantastic primer on Britain's lesser known railways. AA Publishing $29.95

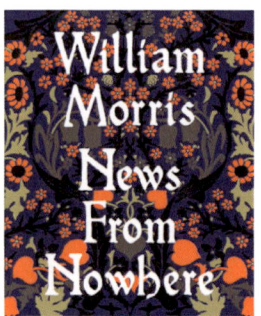

News from Nowhere by William Morris

News from Nowhere caused a stir with its unusual blend of utopian socialism and science fiction when it was first published in installments in William Morris's ideological newspaper The Commonweal in 1890. The Kelmscott Press edition, printed in 1892 and reproduced in this new facsimile edition, was a triumph of book design and making. It's a great look into the mind of brilliant designer William Morris and presents a Utopian vision that we can all aspire too. A must read for fans of Morris's design work and philosophy. Thames & Hudson $45.00

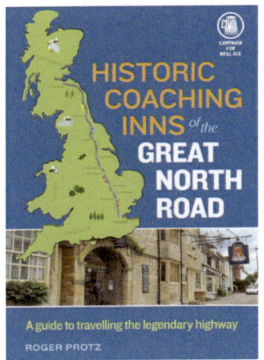

Historic Coaching Inns of the Great North Road

The Great North Road is part of British folklore, the Route 66 of Britain, except instead of gas stations and diners, it has magnificent coaching inns, part of the living history of their islands. Taking in the history of these buildings (including a chapter on highwaymen, who often concealed themselves in secret rooms and tunnels in these inns) as well as the literature that has celebrated them – from Charles Dickens through to J B Priestley – Roger Protz describes these coaching houses with an expert and discerning eye, producing not only a great pub guide but a gazetteer of the history and culture that are draped along this iconic road. This book will prove particularly useful as we plan our drive from the south of Britain to the north next year. It's not just a liting of pubs along the way but inns where you can stay and a look at history you don't normally get from a guidebook. Camra Books $14.99

Canals in Britain by Tony Conder

One of the things on my Britain Bucket List is to rent a restored Canal Boat and explore Britain's network of canals by boat. We had a taste of this experience on the Oxford Union Canal in 2012 and we fell in love. It's such a sedate and enjoyable way to explore Britain. Britain's canals are a vestige of its industrial heritage and while they're no longer used for industry, they're well taken care of as they've become popular with tourists. It could be said that Britain's canals have entered a new renaissance as they've never been more popular than they are now. This fantastic little book from Shire Books is a great overview of the history of the canals and where they stand today. Shire Books $15.00

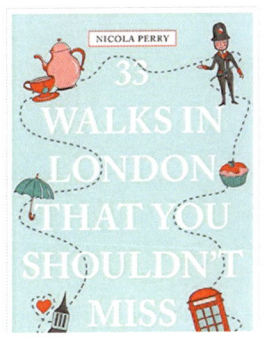

33 Walks in London That You Shouldn't Miss by Nicola Perry

London is the best city in the world for walking. There are hundreds you can take and they're so full of history. So I was pleased to see a fantastic new book from Nicola Perry featuring 33 walks that you shouldn't miss. I agree with every one of her choices. With its labyrinth of characterful streets and alleys, charming squares, open green spaces, monuments and museums, public artworks, bustling markets, and tempting boutiques and restaurants, London is a walker's paradise. Whether you're a first time visitor or longtime local, the city offers endless surprises - fascinating sights and stories, both ancient and modern, hidden in plain view. Features more than 200 pictures and 33 maps, this is the perfect companion for planning London walks. Emons $14.99

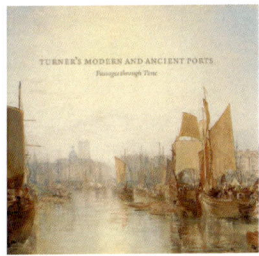

Turner's Modern and Ancient Ports

I'm a sucker for any book about JMW Turner, my favorite British painter. This volume situates J.M.W. Turner's changing (and controversial) technique of the 1820s in the context of his international travels and the profound global transformations then underway. The watercolors and oil paintings that he produced over this period were increasingly focused on the transitional space of the seaport—a space that intimates the passage of time. This beautifully put together book by the Yale University Press was released to coincide with an exhibition that has since ended. The paintings in side are stunning and it's an excellent study of Turner. Yale University Press $45

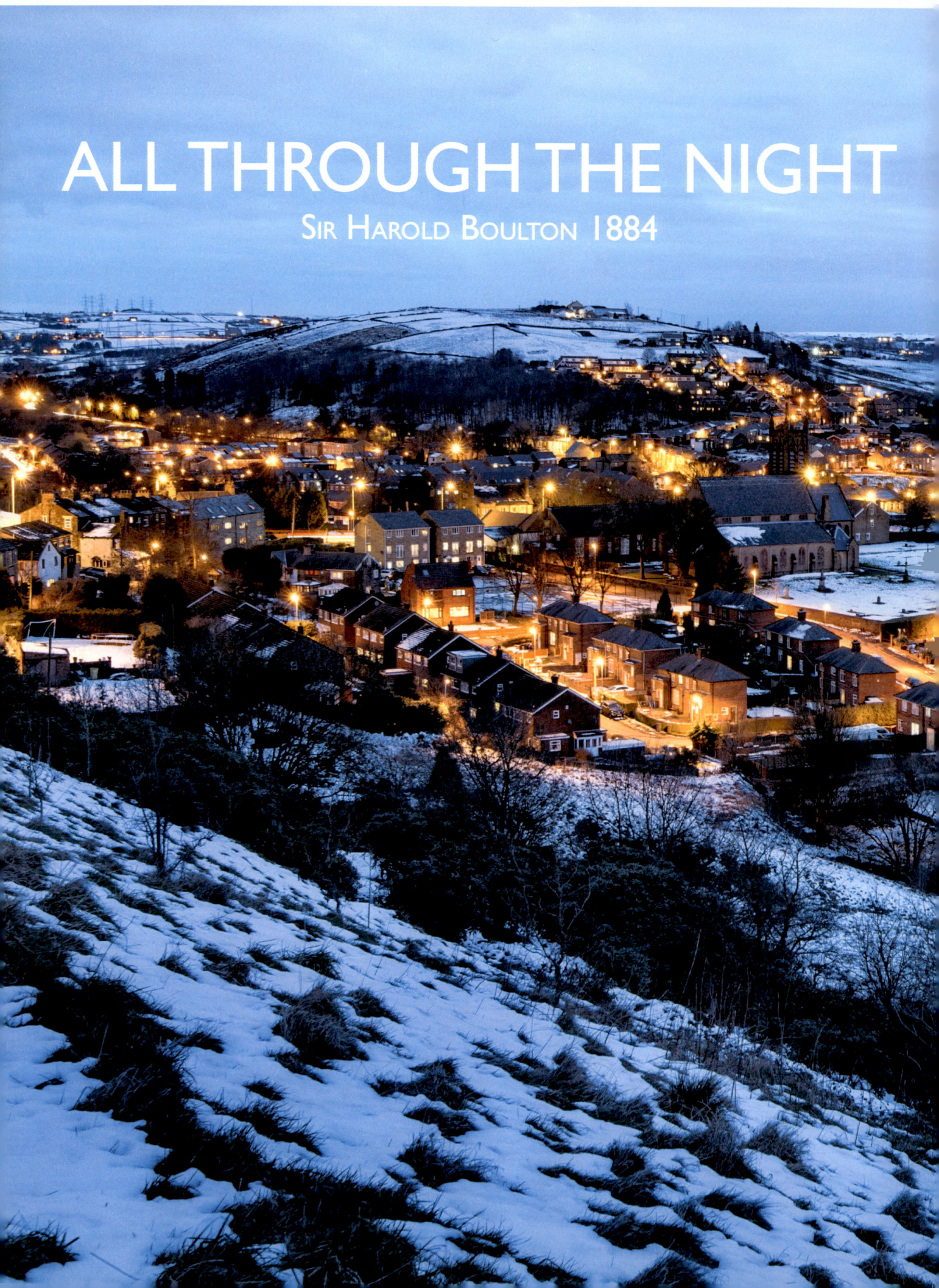

Sleep my child and peace attend thee,
All through the night
Guardian angels God will send thee,
All through the night
Soft the drowsy hours are creeping
Hill and vale in slumber steeping,
I my loving vigil keeping
All through the night.
While the moon her watch is keeping
All through the night
While the weary world is sleeping
All through the night
O'er thy spirit gently stealing
Visions of delight revealing
Breathes a pure and holy feeling
All through the night.

A History of Cadbury
Britain's Favorite Chocolate

John Cadbury began his business career in 1824 as a shop in Birmingham selling coffee, tea, and chocolate. He and his brother soon became manufacturers and adopted the Dutch method of extracting cocoa powder from raw beans. The business expanded under John's son, George, who put into practise his Quaker beliefs by creating a model community and factory – Bournville – designed to provide improved living and working conditions for his employees. Its progressive policies became a model for other model towns. The spectrum of British chocolate treats, as well as powder for 'hot cocoa', flowed from their factory in the early 20th century, and the products are still widely consumed today. The Bournville factory still exists, with other plants around the world. The Bournville model village is a highly desirable place to live, still controlled by the, original Trust set up by George Cadbury. Today the company is completely separated from its family roots, as a subsidiary of Kraft Foods.

Despite its prominence in the English chocolate market today, Cadbury was a 'Johnny-come-lately' in the world of drinking and eating chocolate. In a few decades of the 17th century, all the major non-alcoholic drinks of today arrived in Britain. Coffee was first, followed by drinking chocolate, and simultaneously, tea. Cocoa beans first came to Europe from the New World in 1585. It wasn't long before the drink was a sign of refinement among the wealthy in their palaces. It was so valuable that it was included in the dowries of the Spanish Royal Families.

Only a little later, in 1657, an unnamed Frenchman opened the first chocolate shop in Queen's Head Alley, off Bishopsgate Street in London. He offered samples, lessons, and of course was happy to sell his excellent West India drink. This was just five years after the arrival of coffee, which had already taken off, and chocolate was soon added to the menus of the coffee houses. Tea was first sold in London in the same year as the arrival of chocolate. At that time it was only available as a thick, oily paste made from the ground cocoa beans, sweetened, sometimes flavoured with spices, including chili, and mixed with hot water. The beans sold for 15 shillings a pound, equivalent to £100 today.

When Hans Sloane, who was president of the Royal College of Physicians, when to Jamaica in 1687, he tried chocolate and described it as nauseous. There were numerous recipes for drinking chocolate in circulation at the time, but his recipe mixing it with milk proved popular, even if there were other 'milk chocolate' recipes already in existence. In the 1750s a grocer in Soho, Nicholas Sanders, was selling "Sir Hans Sloane's Milk Chocolate" for medicinal purposes, making it the first brand-name chocolate.

Which lands us very neatly on the doorstep of a shop on Bull Street, Birmingham. There, in 1824, John Cadbury began to sell coffee, tea, and drinking chocolate. Even then, almost 65 years after Mr. Sanders product first appeared, Cadbury was selling tins of drinking chocolate advertised as based on Sloane's original recipe.

Shortly after their store opened, the processing of chocolate underwent a revolution. In 1828 Coenraad Johannes van Houten, a Dutchman, invented a press that would remove the oily cocoa butter from the crushed seeds, leaving behind a de-fatted chocolate powder. This mixed much more easily with milk or water, making home consumption simpler and leading to the sale of 'cocoa', as the English still call it. Not only that, by adding back just some of the cocoa butter, a solid could be made, creating chocolate as we know it today, and making it possible to make chocolate bars.

In 1831 John Cadbury moved from retailer to manufacturer, creating a factory in Bridge Street, Birmingham and producing a range of cocoa and drinking chocolate products. In 1847 he partnered with his brother Benjamin, and they became "Cadbury Brothers". The Cadbury family were Quakers, and as such could not, at that time, study law or medicine, or join the military, which might have been more attractive options to a wealthy family than the competitive world of business. So it is perhaps not surprising that John's son, Richard Barrow Cadbury, took over the retail business in 1850 so that John and Benjamin could focus completely on manufacturing. The brothers expanded their Bridge Street factory, opened an outlet in London, and in 1854 they received the coveted Royal Warrant to supply chocolate and cocoa to Queen Victoria.

Key Facts

- Began in 1824 as a shop selling coffee, tea, and drinking chocolate
- Moved to a model factory and village called Bournville
- Socially progressive based on the family's Quaker beliefs
- Invented almost all the iconic British 'candy bars'

The business did not seem to prosper very greatly, and may even have declined, so in 1860 the brothers dissolved their partnership. John was 59 by then, and when his second wife died the following year, he retired altogether. His sons Richard and George took over the business, and in 1879 they moved everything to Bournbrook Hall, a Georgian mansion between the towns of King's Norton and Northfield, in Worcestershire. The site had been carefully chosen to be in a cleaner, more rural area. Practically speaking it was well supplied for transport by the newly-opened Stirchley Street Station on the Birmingham West Suburban Railway, as well as within easy access of the Worcester and Birmingham Canal, which they used to bring cocoa to the new factory.

This period in the 19th century was blighted by the worst consequences of the untrammelled rapid expansion of Industrial capitalism. Millions may have been freed from the drudgery of farm labour, but it has only been replaced by harsh labour in Blake's Dark, Satanic Mills. Housing was primitive, cramped and unsanitary, diets were poor, disease was rampant, and neither the industrial nouveau riche or the landed gentry and nobility were interested in social change that might undermine their wealth and privilege. It was left to socialists and fundamental Christians like the Quakers to work for improvements in society, and they did it by political action and direct leadership.

As Quakers the Cadburys felt both a moral obligation and a religious imperative to treat their workers differently. Not only were the factory staff treated with great respect and paid relatively high wages, the working conditions were exceptional, there was a pension scheme and worker-

George Cadbury

management committees, and even a staff medical service. Such conditions would only arise in other places after lengthy battles between determined unions and intransigent owners.

In 1893 George Cadbury purchased 120 acres close to the factory and built, from his own wealth, a model village – Bournville – which in his words would alleviate the evils of modern, more cramped living conditions. Within a few years, guided by the company architect William Alexander Harvey, the estate had grown to 313 cottages and houses on 330 acres. Expansion continued up until WWI, and some further housing was even built after that. The houses were built in the fashionable 'Arts & Crafts' style, which was a social statement in itself, considering the socialism of its founder, William Morris. They had large gardens and up-to-date interiors, and they were to become a touchstone for other model villages that were subsequently developed around Britain.

To encourage healthy living, playing fields were built for football and hockey, and in 1924 Rowheath Pavilion was erected to Cadbury's specifications. It included changing rooms, bowling greens, a fishing lake and an outdoor swimming pool. The water came from a pure mineral spring on the site. Membership was entirely free to all staff at the Cadbury factory. In 1900, planning and management of the estate was put into the hands of the fully-independent Bournville Village Trust, still operating today.

Perhaps there was a certain air of benevolent paternalism to the Bournville project. If there was, it was most apparent in the absence of that great British institution, pubs. As a Quaker, Cadbury promoted temperance, and even today there is no pub in the suburb, because of a strict covenant he imposed, although there is a bar for members in the Rowheath Pavilion.

During all this period the company business grew. In 1897, they produced the first milk chocolate bar, a new style developed in Switzerland. The early 20th century saw the development of almost all of their most iconic products. Cadbury's Dairy Milk, in its instantly-recognizable purple wrapper, was launched in 1905, and with a higher milk content, it became their best-selling product by 1914. Bournville Cocoa, in the orange tin, was released in 1906. By 1910, they surpassed their rival Fry, and when WWI began, they were exporting 40% of their sales, chiefly to British outposts in Australia, Canada, New Zealand and South Africa.

In 1915, they expanded from bars to filled chocolates, launching Cadbury's Milk Tray. During WWI 2,000 workers joined the Army (although Quakers were pacifists), and the company sent clothing, books and of course chocolate to them and other soldiers as well. As the war ended their first overseas plant, in Hobart, Tasmania, opened. 1919 saw a merger with their rival J. S. Fry & Sons, bringing Fry's Chocolate Cream and the schoolboy's delight Fry's Turkish Delight into the Cadbury fold.

New products continued to flow from the factories, with Cadbury's Flake in 1920, Cream-filled Eggs in 1923, the Fruit and Nut bar in 1928, and the Crunchie bar in 1929. 1933 saw the arrival of Whole Nut Chocolate Bars, and a permanent place for Cadbury's on the palates of the English was assured. Chocolate was no longer a luxury product, and 90% of the population could afford to eat it regularly.

With chocolate declared an 'essential food' in WWII, the company was placed under government supervision, and rationing did not end until 1950, due to sugar shortages. Parts of the Bournville

factory produced non-lethal war equipment, and the playing fields were ploughed up for food production. In the post-war years, manufacturing expanded both at home and abroad, with factories in Bombay and a major acquisition into the Australian market.

In 1969, they merged with Schweppes, ending the links with the Quaker Cadbury family, and turning the company into a hard-nosed capitalist enterprise. New products followed, most notable the Caramel bar, and with their British business dented by competition from Rowntree, they reduced their product range from 78 to 33. They took 10% of the US chocolate market by their acquisition of Peter Paul. In 2010, following an attempted hostile takeover, Cadbury, now minus the apostrophe 's', was bought by Kraft Foods for £11.5 billion. The takeover was viewed badly by the British public, and by Cadbury staff, and resignations and closures followed swiftly. Today Cadbury is a subsidiary of Mondelēz International, Kraft's confectionary division.

Sites to Visit

- Cadbury bars can be found in every grocery store, but to enjoy the experience to its fullest they should be purchased in a local newsagent's, that British institution selling newspapers, magazines, chocolate bars, potato chips and tobacco products.
- Cadbury's model town of Bournville has been absorbed as a suburb of Birmingham. A drive through the area shows the town-planning and many of the original homes and facilities. Property there is highly coveted.
- The Rowheath Pavilion still exists, although the swimming pool has gone. It is run by volunteers. Heath Road, Bournville, Birmingham, B30 1HH.
- Cadbury World is a park and attraction in Bournville, with self-guided tours, children's activities and exhibitions. Linden Rd, Bournville, Birmingham B30 1JR. There is a parallel centre in Dunedin, New Zealand.

A Very British Christmas
Unique Christmas Events All Around Britain
By Jonathan Thomas

Harbor Christmas Lights in Mousehole, Cornwall

Britain practically invented many of the ways we celebrate Christmas (there's a great article in our Christmas issue last year about how the Victorians Iinvented Christmas). So, it stands to matter that they would have some fantastic events going on throughout the holiday season. As visitors to Britain we love experiencing something that we would not be able to experience back home and the Christmas season is particularly special as Stately homes, and small villages prepare to celebrate the holiday season. We've scoured the island of Great Britain for some events that you should definitely check out if you happen to be there during the holiday season.

Christmas Markets
Cities All Over Britain
Dates Vary Based On Market

What's more 'British Christmas' than a German-style Christmas market? Most major British cities now put on a Christmas market that is modeled on the famous ones held every year in Germany. It's a great way to buy local produce and handmade gifts that you would not be able to find anywhere else. It's important to zero in on the market you want to visit as you will have to plan in advance. These markets are VERY popular and will be very crowded on peak days. Personally, we recommend the Bath Christmas market, it's really quite special to sip some local mulled wine while you browse market stalls setup amongst Bath's beautiful Georgian buildings.

Mousehole Christmas Lights
Mousehole, Cornwall
16 December - 6 January

This yearly display in the Cornish fishing village of Mousehole has put them on the map. The lights are a stunning sight, with floating displays of lights in the harbor and around the streets that are filled with the aroma of mulled wine and festive food. You'll see a fantastic display of sea serpents, fishing boats and whales colorfully lighting up one of Cornwall's most welcoming harbors. The centrepiece is the millennium Celtic cross on St Clement Island, powered ever so greenly by a wind generator. The village is ablaze with color while the lights are on and to really appreciate the displays, walk around the narrow streets and follow the winding strings of lanterns as they disappear around the corner into yet another street barely wide enough to walk through. Have a browse around the local gift shops and stop for a meal and a drink in one of village restaurants, cafes or pubs.

Trafalgar Square Christmas Tree Lighting
Trafalgar Square
First Thursday in December

While the Christmas lights will go on across London during November, on the first Thursday in December, there's a small ceremony to switch on the lights on the Trafalgar Square Christmas tree. There is then carol singing around the tree most nights before Christmas Day. A tree has been donated by to the people of Britain by the city of Oslo, Norway, each year since 1947 as a thank you for Britain's support of Norway during World War II (the Norwegian King stayed in Britain during the war). This symbol of international friendship is decorated Norwegian-style with the lights hanging vertically. Don't miss it!

Christmas Festival of Lights at Longleat
Longleat House, Wiltshire
November to January

Every winter the unmissable Festival of Light comes to Longleat, the famous country home of the Earl of Bath. These illuminations transform the park into a glowing winter wonderland. It draws inspiration from tales new and old; including popular stories like Little Red Riding Hood, the Nordic influenced Little Mermaid, as well as the local legend of Somerset's 'Gurt Worm' dragon but the theme changes every year. The lights are only open on selected dates from early November through January, and the event will see the iconic Wiltshire Estate transported to a whimsical fairy tale land of imagination, through a series of giant and awe-inspiring illuminated lantern displays. Each lantern has been uniquely conceived by Longleat's in-house design team to create a completely new and immersive literary experience for guests to capture the magic of storytelling. The famous safari park is also open during this time, and there are plenty of things to see and do at the estate - such as ice skating. The great house is often decorated for Christmas as well. Booking ahead is essential.

Christmas Festival of Lights at Longleat

Pantomime
Cities All Over Britain
Usually Between Christmas and New Year's

A Christmas Pantomime is a very British tradition that's a bit hard to define. Panto is a type of musical comedy stage production, designed for family entertainment. It was developed in England and is still performed throughout the United Kingdom, generally during the Christmas and New Year season and, to a lesser extent, in other English-speaking countries. Modern pantomime includes songs, gags, slapstick comedy, and dancing, employs gender-crossing actors, and combines topical humor with a story loosely based on a well-known fairy tale, fable or folktale. Pantos run for a very short time, and usually they're so popular they can afford to bring in celebrities from around the world for a few weeks of work. Most major cities in England will have a Panto, but the ones in London will have the biggest names (and sell out quickly).

Hyde Park Winder Wonderland
November-January
Hyde Park

For more than 10 years, Hyde Park's Winter Wonderland has been spreading the Christmas spirit throughout London. The festival has become a landmark event for Londoners and tourists alike. With humble beginnings as an open-air Christmas market in Hyde Park, Winter Wonderland has since grown into an extravaganza with ice skating, shows, roller coaster rides, street food stalls, festive bars and live music. It is still free to enter the Winter Wonderland grounds and take in the joyous atmosphere. With more than 100 spectacular rides and attractions, it is no wonder why thousands of visitors return to Winter Wonderland each year to celebrate the Christmas season. Enjoy skating around the UK's largest open-air ice rink, have a deep sea adventure in the Magical Ice Kingdom, see thrilling circus shows, world-class ice dancing in Cinderella on Ice and see stunning views across London in the Giant Observation Wheel and much more.

London Illuminations

November-January
Regent St and Oxford Street

Oxford Street and Regent Street are the epicenters of Christmas lights in London. Both are turned on in November, usually to much hype involving a celebrity. The lights stay on at night from November until January, and they usually follow a theme - sometimes they're related to a movie, sometimes not. It depends on who paid for the lights that year. If you want a real treat, hop on a double-decker bus and sit at the top - you'll get an up close and personal look at the lights.

Christmas at Various Stately Homes

November-January

Britain's Stately Homes are usually closed for the winter. Since visitors numbers are low, they take the opportunity to clean the house and perform maintenance while tourists are nosing around. But most of Britain's Stately Homes that are open to the public will open for a few weeks around Christmas. They usually decorate the house - sometimes with a historical theme and generally put on a Christmas show. If there's a particular home you want to visit at Christmas, be sure to book ahead. Visiting great houses during Christmas is very popular since most people are off of work for the two weeks around Christmas and New Years.

Santa at the Harrods Grotto

November-Christmas
87-135 Brompton Road, Knightsbridge, London

Going to see Santa isn't a British Tradition like it is in the USA. It's actually rather difficult to find Santas you can visit in Britain. But in recent years going to see Santa has grown in popularity. The most famous 'Santa' is located at Harrods, the iconic British department store in Knightsbridge. The Brits call him Father Christmas, and he lives in a Grotto at the North Pole. Harrods builds a Grotto every year, and it's very popular - in fact, you have to book tickets in August to get a place, and it sells out quickly!

Christmas at Kew, London, England

November-January
Kew, Richmond, Surrey

Learn to ice-skate against the picturesque background of Kew Gardens, which, each year, delivers a sparkling after-dark experience and a truly festive atmosphere. Fairy-tale meets fantasy in a world of singing trees, larger-than-life flora, ribbons of light, giant baubles, and a flickering Fire Garden. The Palm House leaps into life with a dazzling show of laser beams, jets of light and kaleidoscopic projections. Little ones can catch a glimpse of Santa and his elves at the North Pole village and enjoy a vintage fairground ride. Not so little ones can warm up with some mulled wine or hot chocolate and toast marshmallows around the fire. Sounds like a ton of fun.

Christmas Day in London

Unlike the US, most shops and attractions are closed on Christmas Day, so central London is relatively quiet for this one day of the year. There is also no public transport. Boxing Day is another Bank Holiday in the UK so most businesses may still be closed (though many shops open for sales). London is often deserted on Christmas day, so it's a great chance to go for a wander and see one of the world's largest cities completely empty.

Hogwarts in the Snow

November – February 2019
Warner Bros Studio Tour, Studio Tour Drive, Leavesden WD25 7LR

The Studio Tour's annual festive makeover means Christmas trees lining the Great Hall. The Gryffindor common room is decorated for the season; the finale is a blanket of filmmaking snow covering the majestic Hogwarts castle model. The Studio Tour has embraced the holiday season - they've also held special Christmas meals in the Great Hall. Keep an eye on their website for details as these events sell out very quickly.

LOST IN THE POND
The Culture Shock of an American Christmas
By Laurence Brown

When I was a child, Christmas Day made my heart race. Unparalleled was the rush of waiting for Father Christmas to quietly navigate the chimney in search of mince pies; indescribable the first time I bested my brother in a cracker-pull, winning the coveted prize of a miniature thimble; and awe-inspiring those private moments in which I'd gaze into a bauble and see, staring back at me, a warped version of my pre-adolescent face.

Those early introductions to the magic of Yuletide occurred within the festive confines of my English hometown of Grimsby. And as with most childhood experiences, I confidently believed that all of them carried universal weight—as if every human on Earth knew the simple joy of hearing the bang of a cracker or the schmaltzy melody of Chris Rea's Driving Home for Christmas.

And then, at the grand old age of 26 I left behind the British bubble in which I had been sheltered and moved, with my wife, to America.

It was November 2008. A cluster of indistinct specs on the ground had gradually revealed themselves to be grid-like city blocks, as the plane had descended over Indianapolis. This was my first visual encounter with the latest chapter of my life and a stark reminder of the one I was leaving behind.

Perhaps the most enduring aspect of this image was that the city blocks in question—foreshadowing the coming winter—were a distinct shade of white. Snow of this kind was largely absent from the landscape of England. Its presence here on the streets of Indiana's capital was a not-so-subtle declaration from Mother Nature that America's Midwest was going to be dissimilar to England in almost every way.

And this, I would come to find, included Christmas.

Mere hours into my first Christmas morning in America, I caught myself glancing around for those same old tell-tale signs. I wasn't initially disappointed: the walls of my in-laws' house were lined—in familiar fashion—with green and red tinsel; the tree was topped off with a shimmering star, and people were adorned in ugly jumpers.

Except Americans didn't call them "ugly jumpers"; they called them "ugly sweaters." And nowhere to be heard was Driving Home for Christmas; instead, the airwaves were dominated by unfamiliar ditties such as "Feliz Navidad" and "Grandma Got Run Over by a Reindeer."

Speaking of Christmas-themed animals, the popular dish of choice in the Midwest was not necessarily turkey—synonymous more in the U.S. with Thanksgiving. Indeed, the paltry centerpiece with which my then meat-eating self was presented was ham, something that resembled British ham in no discernible way whatsoever. Depending on the region, this might be substituted with chicken, beef, goose, and even oysters!

The dinner table, indeed, is where the cultural Christmas divide is most abundantly brought into focus. It had never occurred to me, for instance, that Americans did not universally stamp Christmas pudding or mince pies onto their dessert menus. While these are not entirely absent from all holiday shopping carts, they do tend to take a back seat to sweet potato pie, pecan pie, and coconut cake.

Now, this is not to say, of course, that I don't devour my American Christmas food well into Boxing Day. Some habits, no matter how old we get or how geographically displaced, never change. Except there's one tiny detail of this anecdote, I neglected to mention: Americans don't celebrate Boxing Day. On 26 December, unless their employer decrees otherwise, most Americans swap the comfort of the couch for the reality of the workplace. Even the term "Boxing Day" carries little currency in this portion of North America—even as its Canadian neighbors to the north celebrate it with abandon.

And "Boxing Day," as you may have guessed, does not stand alone in the Christmas dictionary of British/American word differences. Take, for example, the name each country gives to that jolly fellow who delivers all of the presents: In America, he is known invariably as "Santa," "Santa Claus," or "Old St. Nick"—all used, for sure, in Britain. However, you will rarely—if ever—catch an American referring to him as Father Christmas.

Moreover, Brits and Americans cannot seem to agree on the location of Father Christmas's homeland. Early on after moving to the U.S., during casual Christmas Eve chatter with my in-laws, I made reference to Santa's long journey from Lapland. Not only was the name "Lapland" met with utter puzzlement—as if to say where is that?—but it was later revealed to me that he resides in the North Pole.

Whichever country is correct on this issue, one thing is for sure: Santa certainly chose a hellishly cold place to call home. And so, as it turns out, did I. Those white city blocks were, by no means, an anomaly in the topographical make-up of Indianapolis. Indeed, the notion of a white Christmas in the Midwest is not so much a naive fantasy but more a brutal reality—depending on how warmly you receive it.

And warmth, as it happens, is ensured by burying yourself in multiple layers of heavy duty clothing—a fashion scenario I was rarely forced to undertake during 26 years of British life. Since the chilling wake-up call of my first American winter, there have been occasions on which I've left the house wearing two jackets, each covering a duo of—dare I say it—sweaters, only to find the cold still creeping in.

All that aside, though, I must admit that while experiencing this new kind of Christmas—this American Christmas—I've actually come to treat it once more with the curiosity of a child. For a time, it made my heart race again. Unparalleled was the rush of seeing lines of houses decked out in abnormal levels of illumination; indescribable the first time I bested my brother-in-law in a snow-shovel race, aided—in part—by having a larger shovel than he; and awe-inspiring those private moments in which I'd gaze into a bauble and see, staring back at me, a warped, American version of Christmas.

Which reminds me: it's about time I prepared for that age-old American tradition of stockpiling Christmas crackers. Oh, wait...

Laurence is a British writer and humorist who lives in the United States. He also hosts the popular web series, Lost in the Pond on YouTube. He has an infuriating habit of taking America to task by pointing out how things are done in the UK. He really needs to stop this behavio(u)r. It's anti-American.

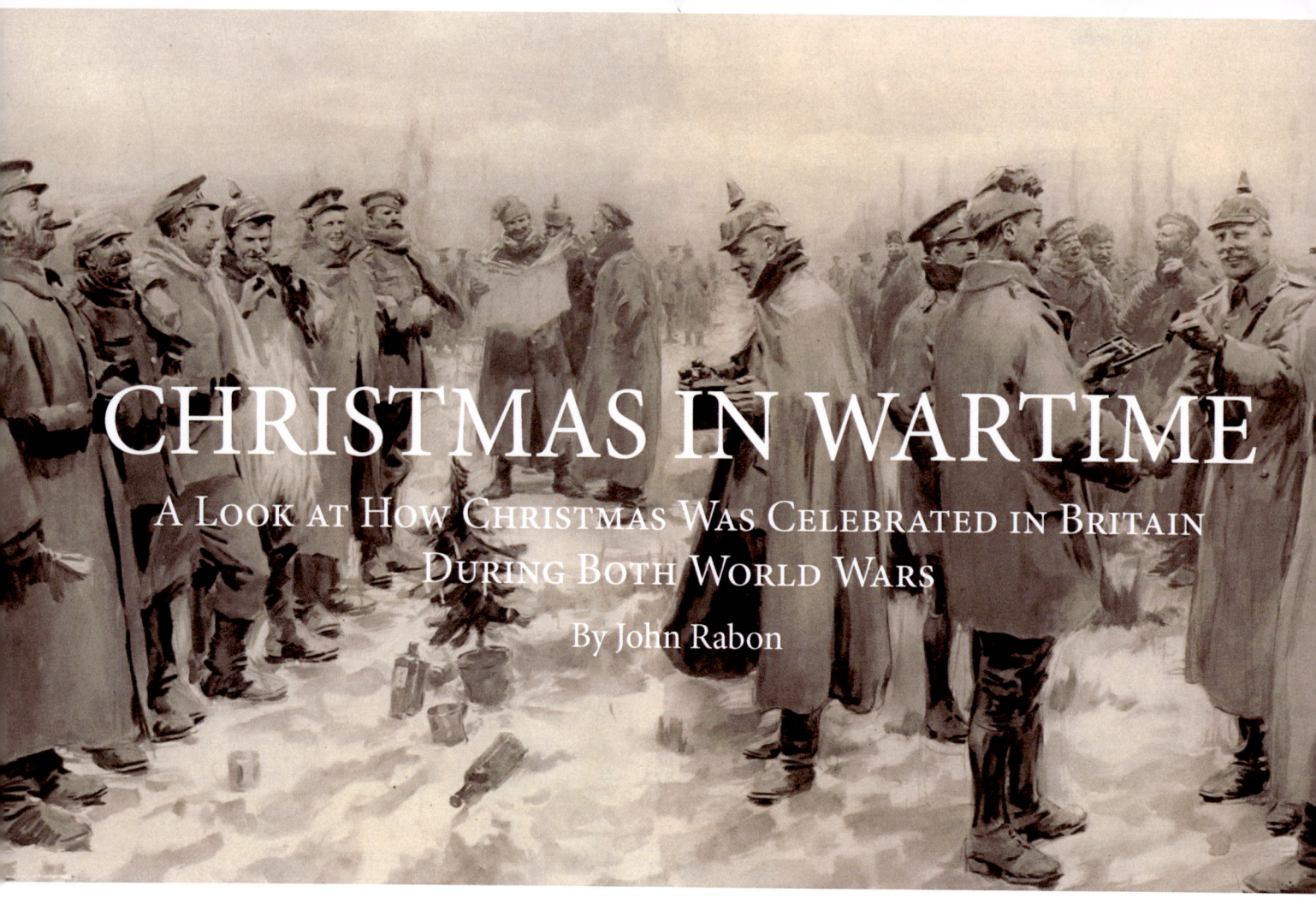

CHRISTMAS IN WARTIME

A Look at How Christmas Was Celebrated in Britain During Both World Wars

By John Rabon

Wartime is not a joyous occasion or a time to celebrate, but the holidays come regardless of whether it's peacetime or wartime. In the midst of the latter, however, it is often necessary to take time away to celebrate and rekindle goodwill within ourselves. This was no truer than in the first half of the 20th century when Britain was involved in two World Wars. Whether on the battlefield or back at home, Christmas celebrations changed with times, and both soldiers and civilians celebrated as best they could. In some cases, this led to innovative new traditions or even near-legendary events.

World War I

When World War I began on 28 July 1914, the consensus was the war would be "over by Christmas". However, within months, it was clear that neither side was gaining the upper hand and the long war of attrition began. Allied forces had managed to stop the advance of the Central Powers and both sides had dug in with trenches established on either side of "No Man's Land", the barren wasteland that would become synonymous with the war itself. "Over by Christmas" then dauntingly transformed into "no end in sight." What followed has been portrayed in countless films from *All Quiet on the Western Front* to 2017's *Wonder Woman*. Trench warfare was particularly brutal. If British soldiers weren't concerned about machine gun fire, snipers, or artillery shells, they had to contend with being exposed to cold, rain, and potential flooding that could bring health risks ranging from pneumonia to "trench foot"—and this was before the use of chemical weapons such as mustard gas.

As December approached, it appeared that Christmas would take place under the shadow of war. In Rome, Pope Benedict XV was the first to suggest a temporary cessation of hostilities for the holiday, but each of the conflicting nations refused to negotiate an official cease-fire. Unofficially, it wasn't unheard of for Allied and Central troops to fraternise on a range from simply collecting the dead every day to even visiting each other's trenches. It was more common for British and German forces to have these interactions than for the Germans and the French, but fraternisation amongst all sides was not uncommon even before Christmas season began.

What became known as the "Christmas Truce" began on 24 December, reportedly by the Germans. German forces began singing Christmas carols in their trenches on Christmas Eve and decorated their trenches with candles and Christmas trees. Soon, British forces also began to sing their own carols and soon enough, the opposing forces were singing to one another. Reports suggest that shortly after this goodwill was established, a German commander sent across a chocolate cake to the British with a note suggesting a cease-fire for the holiday so that the German forces could have a concert. The British accepted and in turn sent back tobacco as their Christmas gift.

With the light of Christmas Day, the Germans were also the first to leave the trenches. British forces feared a trap until they saw that the Germans were unarmed, then came out to meet them. The shaking of hands was followed by the sharing of small gifts in cigarettes, tobacco, plum puddings, and chocolate. Both sides crafted boards that said "Merry Christmas" in English and German. Some reports have impromptu football matches taking place between the two sides. Throughout it all, neither side entered the other's trenches and not a shot was fired. For the most part, the truce remained effective through Boxing Day before the war resumed as normal.

Needless to say, while the soldiers were happy for a reprieve, their commanders were incensed and issued orders against any further fraternisation between the two armies. Any further attempts at a holiday truce were crushed by superior officers and the event never took place again during the war. Of course, this only applied to enemy forces, and the Allies continued to hold Christmas celebrations and more football matches with each other over the war. The first newspaper to publish an account of the truce was The New York Times, at which point the United States was still neutral in the conflict. British papers, including the Daily Mirror, the Daily Sketch, and the Times eventually published accounts that were generally positive, though German newspapers criticised those involved on both sides.

Another special Christmas event in 1914 was the receiving of gift boxes from Princess Mary. The gifts were actually conceived of in October of that year as King George V's daughter wanted to make sure that "every sailor afloat and every soldier affront" should have a present. The princess had wanted to pay for the gifts out of her own private allowance, but it was deemed prohibitively expensive for her, and instead, a public fund was set up that Princess Mary herself oversaw. She crafted a letter that went out across the United Kingdom requesting donations for the gift boxes and her earnest plea greatly helped to fund her plan. Ultimately, each soldier and sailor received a brass box that contained a pipe, tobacco, cigarettes, a Christmas card, and pencil and paper to write home. Many soldiers considered the gift a treasured possession and continued to use it long after the tobacco, cigarettes, paper, and pencil had been used. Other charity organisations sent items such as footballs, harmonicas, books, and even Christmas puddings to the front lines.

Back at home, the war had a different, though noticeable, effect on the Christmas holidays. Shortages of sugar, bread, petrol, and paper were felt amongst people back in the United Kingdom along with the absence of their loved ones. Food shortages, caused both by rationing and naval warfare preventing imports, resulted in some creative recipes come Christmas dinner. Dishes including "celery a la parmesan", which normally would have been a simple side dish of the vegetable sprinkled with a layer of the cheese and baked until crusty, became a featured at holidays meals because of the affordability of ingredients. Chestnuts also became a popular dessert during the war years because they were easy to grow at home.

With the country still engulfed in war as Christmas approached, anything to do with British Expeditionary Forces became popular as a toy item. Toy soldiers, ships, tanks, guns, and uniforms were immensely popular with children. Adults, meanwhile, exercised greater care of their spending and gifts to each other were more practical and affordable. This included care packages sent to loved ones on the western front, and such gifts to soldiers and sailors abroad items such as safety razors, gloves, toolkits, lighters, and other necessities. In addition to 114 million packages sent to troops during the war, letters from home totaled 2 billion, and soldiers delivering mail to the front lines were dubbed "Santa in Khakis".

As the war droned on, soldiers who were not able to return home for the holiday would sometimes spend Christmas in the homes of

Propaganda Poster

French and Belgian civilians they had befriended. While their compatriots at the front might gather together in the trenches to celebrate the holiday and play a bit of footy, soldiers behind the lines from Belgium, France, and the United Kingdom would also celebrate together in the bars and village cafes. Comparatively, Christmas for the Royal Navy was for more ceremonial and traditional, with a religious service followed by Christmas dinner. Of course, the more somber nature of naval celebrations did nothing to damper the cheer and goodwill that the holiday brought to men serving on the cold North Sea and in the Atlantic. Even those wounded in hospital were able to celebrate the holiday as it would aid in their recovery, with decorations and entertainment lifting their spirits. Many of the survivors of the war would not see another Christmas in the United Kingdom until it ended in November 1918, just a month short of the holiday.

World War II

Nearly twenty years later, the world would find itself at war again when Nazi-controlled Germany invaded Poland. With the war beginning in September 1939, there was plenty of time for hostilities to reach the Christmas holidays and the conflict's effects were already being felt by December. While no soldier had yet been killed on the battlefield, conflicts at sea had already claimed the lives of many sailors. At home, Children had been sent away from the cities in fear of bombs that would not drop for months yet and rationing was already in place. The government debated whether to encourage people to conserve their resources and not spend extravagantly for the holidays, but leaders felt that the spending would be good for morale, though the Chancellor of the Exchequer, Sir John Simon, still urged some shrewdness. In the midst of all this, some wealthy citizens were already beginning to feel the pinch as the war cut off their financial resources, and upmarket shops reported the sales of more hampers sent by friends.

Shops did the best they could to encourage people to come in, and with a relative quiet on the western front, many soldiers were actually home mingling with civilians as the purchased gifts for their loved ones. The only thing missing was the children, and toys were purchased for little ones who would not be able to enjoy them for months yet until it was safe to return. As with WWI, war-related toys became popular again including uniforms and Red Cross nurses costumes and even miniature Maginot Lines. Some busses were permitted to carry parents out to the country to visit their children for a day or two. Another wartime gift that became popular again were care packages for soldiers and sailors still abroad, including games, wool clothing, and sweets. As time went on, organisations such as the National Savings Committee encouraged citizens to give money to the war effort instead of purchasing gifts.

Those troops who did find themselves still on the front lines or out at sea were still able to find some of the comforts of the holidays. They would put on their own pantomimes and soldiers still on the homefront but away from their families found themselves welcomed into the homes of nearby

"Blitz-mas" Celebrations in a Bomb Shelter

villagers and townspeople. Soldiers in France were able to enjoy turkey and plum puddings in their modest log cabins but had to stay warm however they could, as fires for forbidden out of fear of giving away their positions. British forces on land during this time were more at risk from frostbite than from the German army, and some had to spend their holiday in hospital.

While the Royal Christmas Message had been twice interrupted since King George V began delivering it in 1932, his son, King George VI, ensured that the message would continue for every year during the war. That first message broadcast over BBC Radio in 1939 was one of reassurance and hope. Thanking the British Expeditionary Forces for their courage and patience, King George also reminded the people that Christmas was a time of peace, and as the nation's future looked uncertain, to put their trust in God. Subsequent messages focused on different themes including separation of families, the efforts made at home to win the war, military victories won by the Allies, and ultimately of peace.

Peace would certainly be a hard thing to find as the war moved into 1940. Only a year after the war began, the event known as the Blitz-ravaged much of Britain, including London, and Christmas was celebrated under a pallour. The last raid had only taken place less than a month beforehand on 15 November and destroyed parts of the National Portrait Gallery, Euston Station, and Westminster Abbey. In the same series of attacks, much of Coventry was destroyed by the Luftwaffe. Only four days after Christmas, 29 December saw the heaviest bombing of the Blitz and was responsible for more than 1,400 fires. It was during this time that the famous photo of St. Paul's cathedral was published in the Daily Mail on New Year's Eve.

Yet those who continued to celebrate made merry despite the circumstances, and many even dubbed the holiday "Blitzmas". Caroling in the streets was cancelled due to the blackout and the inherent danger in being out during the peak time for bombing. While over 1 million Londoners spent the night in air raid shelters, larger shelters held communal Christmas parties with singing, dancing, and skits. In an odd decision, the Christmas classic song "I'll Be Home for Christmas" by American singer Bing Crosby was actually banned by the BBC for being too depressing, as the lyrics described a

Mrs Devereux and her daughter Jean pull a Christmas cracker in front of their Christmas tree at their home donated by the YMCA to families in Britain. © IWM (Art.IWM PST 16433)

soldier who wanted to be with his family for the holiday. The Royal Family's Christmas card that year depicted the Windsors standing outside the bombed section of Buckingham Palace, though they did not celebrate the holiday there. The family's location for Christmas was kept secret to prevent the Nazis from attempting to bomb and kill King George and the future Queen Elizabeth.

With all the doom and gloom hanging around, people all over Britain did the best they could to celebrate. Christmas decorations went up regardless of the potential destruction, and some families even decorated their air raid shelters. Decorations were often hand-made from paper due to the unavailability of ornaments in the shops. Rationing of food was in full effect by this point, beginning in January, and items subject to the rationing included bacon, butter, sugar, and tea. During December, the tea rationed doubled, and the sugar ration was increased by one-third. As the war went on, more items would be added to the rationing list such as eggs, milk, cheese, preserves, and more. Food prices rose during the war and imports from the Continent were non-existent.

Some families received help during the holidays from American troops stationed in the United Kingdom. The Royal Army and the United States Army encouraged the American G.I.s to "[fill] the chairs left empty by British fighting men" and the soldiers were given extra ration packs to take with them for their British hosts. The packs included special items such as evaporated milk, fruit juice, bacon, coffee, sugar, rice, peas, and lard. The exchange proved to be so popular that, in 1942, one American commander estimated that there were fifty invitations per each soldier stationed there. On base, American soldiers would throw their own lavish parties and invite the locals to come celebrate with them, especially the children who had been evacuated from the cities and were far from their own families. The American would even play the role of Father Christmas.

The Ministry of Food each year would release its own recipe suggestions to help everyone prepare Christmas dinner despite the rationing suck as "Mock Goose" which contained no meat or "Mock Turkey" which was really made from lamb. Desserts might include "carrot fudge" or "candied carrots".

Outside of London, many places celebrated as normal as they could. As materials were included in rationing, clothes, toys, and other items made of cotton, metal, and the like became scares and gifts became more practical. Rationing eventually switched to a points system and people would save up their points to provide as much as they could for Christmas dinner, but items became even scarcer as the war drone on. The Ministry of Food even encouraged people to make "vegetable bowls" instead of fruit bowls because the former had "such jolly colours."

Away from home, soldiers and sailors did the best they could to celebrate the holiday, as they had during World War I. For sailors, the days leading up to Christmas included decorating the mess halls and ward rooms with balloons and streamers. Some ships would even raise a Christmas tree to the masthead. The captain would typically read the Christmas service for that day then make his inspection, which was less formal than others and gave him the opportunity to greet and joke with the sailors aboard ship. Lunch was then served that ideally included turkey and plum pudding followed by the crew's rum ration. Ships docked back home were able to enjoy their Christmas spirits a bit more liberally than those at sea, though sailors' accounts imply a heavy amount of drinking in either situation.

Soldiers celebrated the holiday on the front lines, doing their best to make Christmas meals out of what was available and holding church services even as far away as Libya. Christmas Carols would be sung at camp, though how traditional the Christmas dinner was depended on how close to the front lines the soldiers were. Those soldiers who later liberated Italy were able to add some fine Italian wines to their Christmas meals. A lucky few even got leave to return home for the holidays, but it wouldn't be until 1945 that demobilisation would see millions of soldiers and sailors return home for Christmas.

Of course, even though the war was over, its effects lingered through Christmas 1945. Families had to adjust to their "demobbed" relatives returning from the war. As husbands and wives had both changed significantly, there was an adjustment in many British homes during the holidays as they became re-acquainted. Rationing would not end for another nine years, so much of the scarcity that had defined the holiday during the war remained.

A Shelter in Camden Town under a Brewery : Christmas Eve, 1940 © IWM (Art.IWM ART LD 1899)

Christmas chains were made mostly out of newspaper and what Christmas cards existed were often small and printed on very thin sheets. The Ministry of Food still issued its alternative recipes with its "Mock Turkey" or "Murkey" consisting of sausages, breadcrumbs, and vegetables. Toy manufacturers had largely shut down or turned their operations to the war effort, and as many such toys received were hand-made out of wood. Instead of the Americans visiting at Christmastime, it was the Germans as POWs who were working in England before their repatriation who were now invited to share the holiday. It would take some time for Christmas to return to the finery and unencumbered joy it had known before the war.

Despite it all, whether home or abroad, Christmas managed to be a time or joy and peace during the chaos of two world wars. Enemies found fellowship on the battlefield with one another, if only for a day. Though families were separated, they found ways to welcome lonely servicemen into their homes. Even though the means to make merry were scarce, people found a way to make do with what they had and to share it with others. Christmas, no matter what the horrors of war could do, was not and could not be cancelled.

ROBERT WALPOLE
The First Prime Minister

Robert Walpole came to prominence just as power in Britain was shifting from the Crown to the Parliament. He was the first, and the longest serving, Prime Minister under the newly-developed balance of power. Although he ruled more by influencing the King than by using Parliament, he laid the foundations for the present constitutional monarchy. By avoiding wars for an extended period, he allowed the country to grow in wealth and establish itself as a powerful nation, ready to build an Empire. He also personally enriched himself and retained power by using the corrupt political system which existed at that time.

The Glorious Revolution in 1688 was a turning-point in British history, shifting the balance of power away from the Monarch and toward the Parliament. After the English Civil War abolished the Monarchy, Charles II returned to the throne when the Commonwealth collapsed in 1660, but when Charles II died in 1685 his already-unpopular Catholic brother, James II, took the throne. English Protestants were outraged, and a group of nobles arranged for his nephew and son-in-law William, Prince of Orange, to invade England and ensure that a Protestant dynasty ruled. James II fled and William and Mary took the throne, establishing a Protestant succession that has continued in various forms into the present. But William got the throne at a price – The Bill of Rights of 1689.

The Bill of Rights listed 12 things that James had done to subvert the laws and liberties of this kingdom and asserted a list of ancient rights and liberties which were to be protected. These lists repeated used the term without the consent of Parliament, effectively limiting the power of the King in matters such as raising an Army; the election of MPs; levying taxes; establishing fines and punishments; and limiting free speech within Parliament. Britain does not have a written constitution, so the transfer of these powers to Parliament represented a major shift of power towards a constitutional monarchy, such as exists in Britain today.

What the King could still do was select the person who was his Prime Minister, who must, however, be the person most likely to command the confidence of the House of Commons. The first person to effectively hold that position was Robert Walpole, 1st Earl of Orford.

Walpole was born in the small Norfolk village of Houghton on the 26 August, 1676. He was the fifth of what were to become 19 brothers and sisters. His father was a member of the local gentry and an MP for the Whig party. Robert was educated privately and then went on to Eton School and King's College, Cambridge. Although he had intended to enter the clergy, plans changed after his two elder brothers died, leaving him the heir. He returned home to help his father, and two years later, in 1700, his father died, leaving the family estate of 10 manor houses and land to the 24-year-old Robert.

It was relatively easy to take advantage of the corrupt nature of the electoral system of the time – there was no secret ballot and since those eligible to vote were limited, a rich man could buy all the properties with voting rights, install obedient tenants, and ensure a seat for perpetuity – a so-called pocket borough. This Walpole did in 1702 with the borough of Kings Lynn, in the same year that William died, and the popular protestant Queen Anne took the throne. Like his father, he was a Whig, whose rivals in parliament were the Tories. The Whigs were largely responsible for curtailing the freedom of the monarch, preferring to exercise power themselves. Their political descendants became the current Liberal Party. They supported Protestantism and were largely responsible for the Glorious Revolution.

Walpole caught the eye of the new Queen and became a member of the advisory council to her husband, Prince George of Denmark. He entered the Cabinet of Lord Godolphin as Secretary of War and Treasurer of the Navy. When power shifted to the Tories at the election of 1710, the new Lord High Treasurer was a defector from the Whigs, Robert Harley, who attempted to entice Walpole to join him, but failed, leaving Walpole as a major critic

Key Facts

- Born 1676 – died 1745
- Britain's first Prime Minister
- Established the foundations of the British parliamentary system
- Kept his party – the Whigs – in power for 50 years

of the new government and defender of the Whig cause. To eliminate him from the opposition he was found guilty of accepting bribes and expelled from Parliament. He spent six months as a prisoner in the Tower of London, where he continued to attack the government, but in 1713 he was re-elected to his seat of Kings Lynn.

The death of Queen Anne the following year brought her distant German cousin, George I, to the throne, a triumph for the Whigs, we retained power for the next 50 years. Walpole became a powerful member of the Cabinet as a Privy Councillor and Paymaster of the Forces. He also condemned without trial prominent members of the previous Tory government. He quickly rose to Lord of the Treasury and Chancellor of the Exchequer. In a dispute over foreign policy with other cabinet members Walpole chose to resign and join the opposition, but after being influential in ending a rift in the royal family, he returned to the Cabinet.

As a younger man, Walpole had purchased shares in the South Sea Company, a joint-stock company with a monopoly on trade with South America. Walpole enjoyed a 1,000% profit, but others were not so fortunate, and when the highly inflated value of the stock began to fall in the event known as the South Sea Bubble, prominent cabinet members were implicated. Although Walpole protected them from punishment, he benefited from their resignations and was able to eliminate several long-standing rivals, leaving him the most prominent and powerful figure in the Cabinet. He simultaneously became First Lord of the Treasury, Chancellor of the Exchequer and Leader of the House of Commons; with his brother-in-law Lord Townsend by his side they effectively controlled the entire government. He became, in fact, if not in the title, the King's 'Prime Minister', the first since the Glorious Revolution established the importance of such a position. He devised a scheme to partially repay those most injured by the South Sea debacle, and reduced the damage to the reputation of the King and the Whig party.

Throughout the reign of George I the power of the Cabinet and the Prime Minister rose, as that of the King declined. When George II took the throne, he retained Walpole and even Townsend, despite a personal dislike of him. When Townsend died in 1730, Walpole was left in sole charge and clearly the most powerful person in the country. Despite opposition and ridicule from many social liberals, like Jonathan Swift and Dr Samuel Johnson, Walpole was able to remain popular with the people by keeping Britain out of wars and thus keeping taxes low. Despite a succession of crises he retained power, even managing to silence critics like Alexander Pope and Henry Fielding by regulating the theatres, so reducing their power to parody and satirise him.

As time passed, however, his popularity waned, and an unsuccessful war with Spain further damaged his reputation. Finally, corruption and his immense personal enrichment led to a parliamentary inquiry and rather than face the outcome he resigned from office, ending his political career. Always one to land on his feet, however, George II, grieving at the loss of his favourite minister, made him Earl of Orford, thus giving him a seat in the House of Lords. He continued to wield considerable influence with the King, and became known as the 'Minister behind the Curtain'. As he grew older, he retreated more and more to his country estate, to hunt and admire his extensive collection of art, acquired during his years of power. However his health continued to deteriorate, and he died on the 18 March, 1745.

His Legacy

Although usually regarded as Britain's first Prime Minister in the modern sense, in fact, Walpole governed more by personal influence with the King than by using the House of Commons. He did, however, reduce the Tories to insignificance and ensure Whig dominance for half a century. By keeping Britain away from the older pattern of perpetual wars, he greatly enriched the country, doing that also by protectionist trade policies that allowed the wool industry to thrive and produce revenue for necessary imports.

The use of 10 Downing Street as the official residence of the Prime Minister also dates back to Walpole's time. The house was a personal gift to him from George II, although he only used it as his residence when he was First Lord of the Treasury. As for corruption and personal gain, he was probably no more corrupt than most of his peers, although he was known to advise new MPs the rid themselves of their principles and become 'wiser'.

Sites to Visit

- Walpole is buried in his family vault in St Martin Churchyard, Houghton, Norfolk.
- There is a statue of Walpole in St. Stephen's Hall, Palace of Westminster (the Parliament Building).
- There is a blue plaque on a house where Walpole lived, at 5 Arlington Street, Westminster, SW1.

Further Research

- The Great Man: Sir Robert Walpole: Scoundrel, Genius and Britain's First Prime Minister, by Edward Pearce
- Sir Robert Walpole, by B. W. Hill
- Walpole, by John Morley
- Sir Robert Walpole: A Political Biography, 1676-1745, by Alexander Charles Ewald
- Walpole and the Whig Supremacy, by H. T. Dickinson

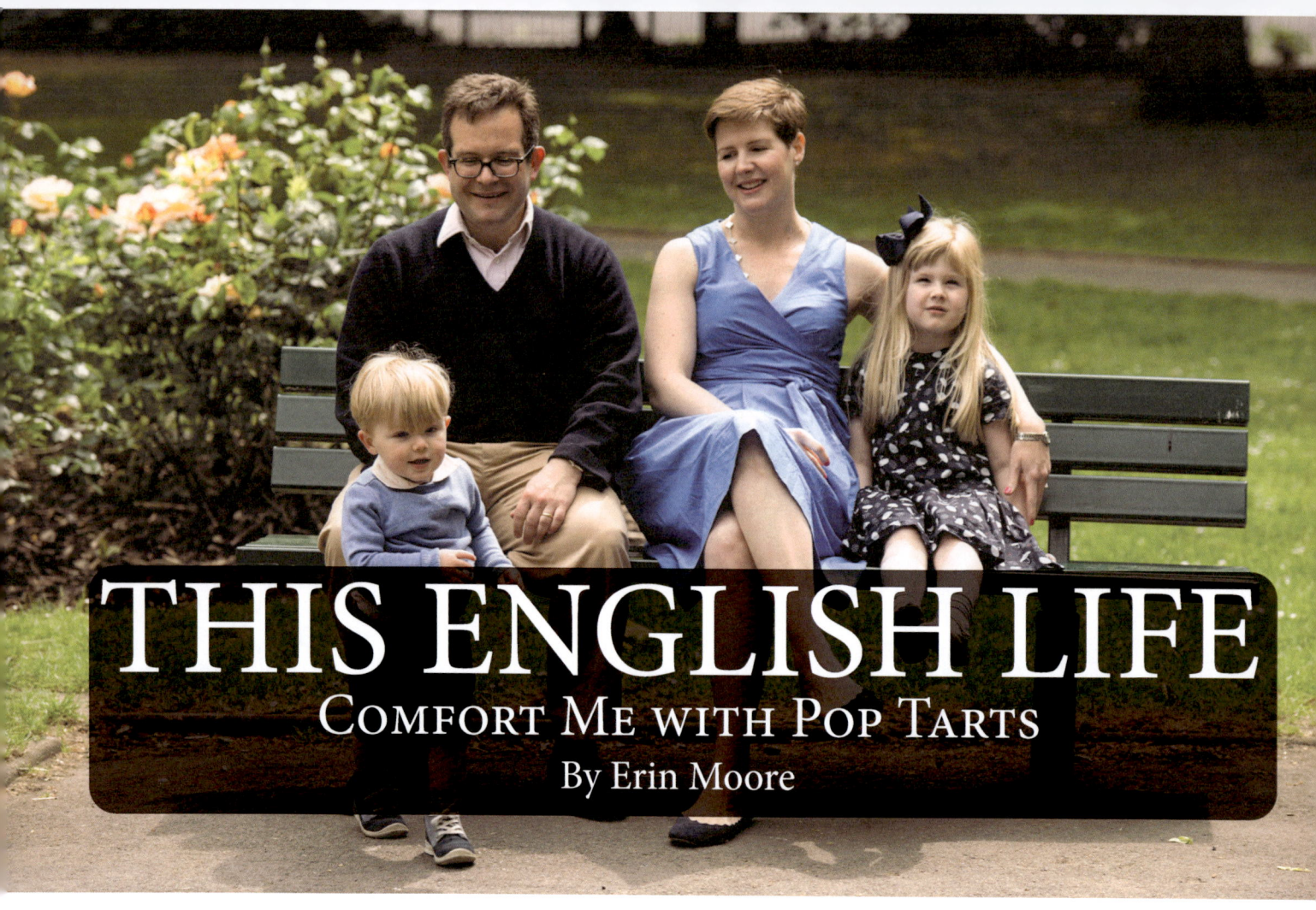

THIS ENGLISH LIFE
Comfort Me with Pop Tarts
By Erin Moore

At her school's annual fete, Anne and I are trying to guess the number of marshmallows in a jar. I don't particularly want Anne to win the marshmallows, but I can't resist approaching it as a math problem—sorry, a math opportunity.

We first imagine how many of the small pink cylindrical marshmallows would fit in Anne's hand; then, how much of the jar that one handful would fill, and how many handfuls it would take to get to the top. When we have our number, we write it down and skip off to the bouncy castle. We are surprised, hours later, to find out that Anne's guess was exactly correct, to the marshmallow.

Anne loves marshmallows, but I convince her it will be more fun to give them away to her friends by the handful than hoard them at home. We walk back through the crowd, greeted like heroes, passing them out to kids who are already sticky from cotton candy (called Candy Floss here) and ice cream cones. The last 20 or so will make their way to our pantry and sit in a bag until a month later when they make a handy bribe for potty training my youngest. Years from today, will he find that every visit to the men's room brings on an inexplicable marshmallow craving? If so, he will have me to blame. I still remember when my brother made the lucky guess on a 5-liter jar of jelly beans when we were kids. Of course, the big winner was our dentist.

Ten years after moving to London, and 23 years after leaving my family home in Florida, I don't get homesick very often. But when I do, my feeling of longing is not for a place; it's for familiar people—the best people—and nostalgic foods, the worst foods. (Find me someone who longs for enemies and celery. I'll wait...) Sometimes books help get me through these feelings more reliably than anything else. My daughter and I are working our way through the Ramona Quimby stories. Last summer, we read the first six Nancy Drews (until all the plots started to run together and we took a break). The year before that, it was the Anne of Green Gables books. But so far the biggest hit of my childhood library has been Roald Dahl.

We have just finished re-reading "Charlie and the Chocolate Factory". The book has me thinking about the outsized role of candy in a child's imagination. When we got to the part about how Charlie was so poor that he only got to eat one bar of chocolate each year, on his birthday, Anne's breath caught audibly in her throat. For Anne, candy is more a once a week sort of treat, but she and her friends spend a lot of time thinking about it anyway. So did Dahl, who ate a Cadbury bar after lunch every day and saved the foil wrappers, one rolled around the next, until they resembled a cannonball. You can Google it if you want to see a picture because it's now part of the permanent collection at the Ronald Dahl Museum.

Anne's friend Matilda, who has visited the US before, is particularly fascinated by American candy, which in her mind is of limitless variety and (ironically) Willy Wonka-style inventiveness. She describes in salivating detail the American candies she knows, like Twizzlers, and she loves to invent her own candy bar combinations and ask me if they exist "in America." And I'll say, "No—but listen to this!" Then I describe my favorites and watch the kids' faces register delight (Almond Joy, Snickers) or disgust (Peppermint Patties, Atomic Fireballs).

Because they are 7, and the daughters of health-conscious mothers, what Anne and Matilda love most are the real tooth-achers: Jolly Ranchers, Nerds, Starburst. But Anne may be alone among 7-year-olds in not understanding the purpose of chewing gum. The first time a friend gave her a piece, she put it in her mouth and chewed for a minute, then bent over and started spitting on the ground to get rid of the taste. Anne got really mad when everyone laughed.

Although I don't chew it much anymore, in my experience American kids are born knowing how to chew gum, and don't require lessons. This wasn't the first clue that Anne gave me that she is actually an English child. The first time she saw ice water, at age two, she asked what was floating in it. Sometimes I feel conflicted about the cultural experiences she is missing out on.

I adore British candy, and if you check my suitcases on the way out of the Heathrow you will find all the sweets I am sharing with my American family and friends: Cadbury Dairy Milk, chocolate buttons, Smarties (like M&Ms, but the orange ones have orange-flavored shells), Flake Bars, and Bendick's Bittermints (my and my parents' favorite). But if you check my bags on the way home, the Toll House Morsels, Peppermint Patties, and peanut butter M&Ms are mostly, as they say on the customs forms, for my own use. Sometimes, when homesickness hits, books aren't enough.

A few weeks later, on my way to the gym (anyone with a sweet tooth like mine has to atone for it somehow), I notice a new shop. Chaotically, thrillingly colorful and stocked to the rafters with American junk food—all of the tastes of my childhood, plus. Not only Oreos but birthday cake-flavored Oreos. Not just Jell-O but Jolly Rancher flavored Jell-O. M&Ms in flavors I love already—peanut butter, almond, mint—and flavors I never imagined. Pretzel? Yes, please. Coffee? Bleurgh!

Then, I see the Pop Tarts. They have every kind, but my eyes find Strawberry right away. I haven't eaten a Pop Tart in 20 years at least, maybe twenty-five! I buy a box, along with pretzel M&Ms and cherry Jell-O that will endear me to every kid on Anne's next play date. The total comes to an eye-watering 14 pounds—about $18—but I'm so eager to introduce Anne to the nostalgic flavors of my childhood, I don't even care. When we were in college, my half-English husband once hosted a "Low Tea," serving Twinkies, Oatmeal Cream Pies, Entenmann's Coffee Cake and powdered donuts. Our tastes were still childish back then, and I'm afraid my palate hasn't matured much.

I already know my son, Henry, won't be trying any of these treats because he is, to put it mildly, a conservative eater. I have one child who has been slurping down raw oysters since the age of three and prefers her shrimp to be served with the heads on so she can suck the brains. Her little brother will go on a 24-hour food strike if you serve him the wrong pasta shape. They both have a sweet tooth like their mother, but I'm not optimistic about Henry and Pop Tarts. Anne's Dad introduced her to shellfish. It's one of many special things they like to eat together. Pop Tarts can be ours.

Back at home the next morning, I unveil the Pop Tarts with real ceremony. Anne is suitably impressed. Is she actually about to be offered what appears to be a plate-sized frosted biscuit full of jam FOR BREAKFAST? Yes, yes she is. Let me tell you, a strawberry Pop Tart is my Proustian Madeleine. It comes out of the toaster hot, Hot, HOT and I juggle it to the plate. As I taste it, my thoughts travel immediately to the other six packs of two in the box on the counter. This is going to be trouble. Oh, well, probably best if I eat most of them, as they might stunt Anne's growth...

My greedy reverie is interrupted by the voice of

an outraged child. "YUCK! THIS IS DISGUSTING! Mom, you eat mine, okay?" Anne hadn't spit her first bite of Pop Tart out, but she'd pushed her plate away, and the look on her face was eloquent. Anne would rather have a nice buttered crumpet or even a bit of baguette with butter and a wedge of comté. She loves bagels. (We can buy them on Brick Lane, but only the plain kind. The rainbow bagel and the everything bagel have not made their way here yet. I miss sesame.) She even appreciates a pancake with butter (a theme emerges) and maple syrup, but days later, she will still be talking about how putrid Pop Tarts are. Pop Tarts are apparently not going to be our thing.

We have a rule in our house that no one is allowed to ridicule anyone else's food preferences. We all break it constantly. Anne will cross the kitchen to escape the aroma of Henry's apricot yogurt. Anne and Tom like to visit London's many cheese shops and skulk home with great wedges of Stinking Bishop, Stilton and rank rounds of goat cheese. Which they eat with relish, as Henry and I retire to the far end of the house. Tom likes cheese-flavored crackers which smell like feet. Dry sausages redolent of a barnyard that could use a good mucking-out.

I myself can clear a room with my alarming-looking green algae shots, kombucha with skeins of live and active bacteria floating within, and "ice cream" made of cashews and coconut. I still have a soft spot for real junk, though, and those Pop Tarts are calling to me every day. Maybe I'll invite Matilda over and give them to her. If anyone can understand their pink appeal, she can. I know it.

About the Author

Erin Moore is an American who has been living in London for 10 years. Her book, That's Not English: Britishisms, Americanisms and What Our English Says About Us, is available on amazon.com.

BOXING DAY 101
What is it and how do you celebrate?
By Jonathan Thomas

When Americans first try to read up on British Christmas traditions, they're often confused by Boxing Day, which always falls the day after Christmas. It's not a religious holiday and there's nothing to actually celebrate. So, what exactly is it and what is it for? Well, fear not, we will try to lift the shroud of mystery and show you what it's all about.

It's Basically An Extra Day Off

The main thing that sets Boxing Day apart from all the other holiday is that it's basically another day off after Christmas. In Britain, Boxing Day is always a Bank Holiday which means banks are closed are most retail stores are required to have limited hours (usually up 6 hours open by law). In the USA, many people go right back to work the day after Christmas. Having another day to recoup the madness of the holidays is so much more civilized.

Started Off As A Servants Holiday

There are competing theories for the origins of the term, none of which is definitive. The Oxford English Dictionary gives the earliest appearances from Britain in the 1830s, defining it as "the first week-day after Christmas-day, observed as a holiday on which post-men, errand-boys, and servants of various kinds expect to receive a Christmas-box." In Britain, it was a custom for tradespeople to collect "Christmas boxes" of money or presents on the first weekday after Christmas as thanks for good service throughout the year. This custom is linked to an older British tradition: since they would have to wait on their masters on Christmas Day, the servants of the wealthy were allowed the next day to visit their families. The employers would give each servant a box to take home containing gifts, bonuses, and sometimes leftover food. Now, it's a holiday for everyone, but gifts are no longer exchanged.

Famous For Its Sales

In America we have Black Friday Sales, in Britain, they have Boxing Day Sales, which is usually the biggest shopping day of the year in the UK as people rush to the stores to snag great deals and return the gifts they didn't want. It's a great way for retailers to clear out the stock they have leftover from the Christmas shopping binge. The deals have moved online in recent years, but you will find Britain's stores and malls (shopping centers) heaving on Boxing Day, but only for the 6 hours they're allowed to be open. Deals can be had if you can brave the crowds.

Boxing Day Lunch

Sunday Roast is a venerable British tradition, and many families will extend it to include Boxing Day, even if it's not on a Sunday. Sometimes they'll eat a roast, or they'll eat a lunch of leftovers from the previous day's Christmas Feast. Pubs are usually open, so you can go get a nice meal as well. It's a time for families and friends to spend the day together without the pressures of work and school.

A Day for a Stroll

Many of Britain's tourist attractions that are usually closed for the winter will open up for the period between Christmas and New Year's. This includes many famous Stately Homes that will have special opening hours. So, Boxing day is a great day to go out for a walk in Britain's beautiful countryside and enjoy some famous buildings while you're at it.

Simply put, Boxing Day is a day to enjoy the joys of the mid-winter break from the rat race. To eat good food, get a good deal or spend time with your friends and family. It's certainly a lesson we can all learn from!

MAKE YOUR CHRISTMAS MEAL BRITISH
SCRUMPTIOUS TRAIDITIONAL BRITISH DISHES TO TRY THIS YEAR

By John Rabon

For centuries, even before it was a Christian holiday, Christmas was a day of feasting. In fact, during the Protectorate period, Oliver Cromwell banned Christmas feasts and ordered his soldiers to seize any meals prepared for the holiday. He was the first Christmas Scrooge. In America, there are a lot of traditional meals that we share with our cousins across the pond, but there are certainly a few differences. While you might find turkey, ham, roasted potatoes, and cake in both countries, Britain has a few Christmas meal traditions that are quite different. Here are five of our favorites you have to try and incorporate into your Christmas dinner. Based on recent travel experience, you won't regret trying any of these!

Pigs in a Blanket

Yeah, we have those in America, you think, but not like they do it in Britain. The American version and the British version both start with one basic ingredient, sausages, but that's where it ends. While Americans put the sausages in rolls of dough, Britain wraps them in bacon. Yes, bacon. It seems that we've been doing it wrong all these years or Pillsbury has some really good marketing. You better believe that I'm going to be giving this a try at the holidays this year. The British really do know how to do things properly. And by properly I mean wrap something in bacon.

Roasted Parsnips

Parsnips aren't as popular here, but in the UK the root vegetable that is in the same family as carrots is a regular dish at the holidays. If you want to include them amongst your dishes this holiday, there are many ways to prepare them, but roasting them seems to be among the top favorites. If you want, you can serve them with carrots, glazed in honey, with sweet potatoes, or any combination you choose. However you choose, it's usually best to slice them to cook them thoroughly and impress your guests with your culinary skills. They will certainly add some very interesting new flavors to your big Christmas feast.

Mince Pies

Something not known to most Americans even

though they might be familiar with dessert pies such as peach, apple, and blackberry. Mince pies are different in that they're typically much smaller and a mixture of fruits and spices. They can contain such fruits as black currants, raisins, sultanas, apricots, cherries, and apples as well as typically cinnamon and nutmeg. This combination is also known as mincemeat, from which the pie derives its name. For dessert, most families will pick between them or another entry on this list, but you can even have both if you feel so inclined. It takes a lot of skill to make them yourself (we featured a great recipe in our last Christmas issue) but most Brits will just pick them up from the grocery store. Loyalty to your particular brand of mince pie is tantamount to a religion to the British. Don't mess with mince pies. You've been warned!

Bread Sauce

Its recipe dates back to the Medieval period; it's possibly the oldest Christmas dish on this list. During that time, cooks typically used bread to thicken sauces, and the leftovers eventually became a popular dish on their own. Bread sauce is usually made with quite a few ingredients such as: bread crumbs, milk, butter or cream, and sometimes onion, salt, cloves, mace, pepper, bay leaf, or even animal fat. Today, you can make bread sauce either to drop over your meats and stuffing or just enjoy it on its own. However you choose to serve it, you'll truly have a British Christmas with it on your Christmas feast table.

Christmas Pudding

The top Christmas dessert, Christmas pudding can describe either a sweet or savory dish, though it's typically sweet for the holiday. Many families have their own traditional recipe that's been passed down for generations but typically consists of suet, black treacle, and dark sugars, though some people will throw raisins or black currants in there as well. Most recipes also include some kind of rum drizzle or another icing over the top. In old times, the pudding was made before the beginning of Advent and aged until Christmas Day. Of course, you don't have to wait that long to make yours, and you can find most of the ingredients in the grocery store.

GREAT BRITISH ICONS: PENGUIN BOOKS

By David Goodfellow

Penguin Books began in 1935 in the bathroom of three brothers, who devised the idea of publishing quality books at low cost. Using modern graphics and printing methods, they created the paperback format in its modern form and brought low-cost books to a mass market. The founder, Allan Lane, was known for his dictatorial control of the company, considerably business acumen and a propensity for publishing controversial books for publicity as well as principle. The company thrived during WWII but declined in the face of growing competition during the post-war years. It ended as an independent company in 1970, following the death of Allan Lane.

Social visionaries of the 19th century saw very early that education for everyone was a vital engine of social change. While the majority of the population remained illiterate, or limited to the most basic skills, social improvement would remain a dream. Education was not free and was thus out of the reach of the children of the poorest workers, who made up much of the population. So an important aspect of most groups, motivated by religion or socialism, was to raise the standards of education. Classes in adult education for working people developed in the middle of the 19th century with the Working Men's College and the Working Women's College, later to become the Worker's Educational Association, grew on the principle of education for everyone. Self-education too became a goal for many, and it was with that goal that publisher Joseph Dent, himself an autodidact, founded the Everyman's Library in 1906. This was a series of 50 classical books, reprinted, in a pocket-sized format, made with low-cost methods and sold for one shilling (one 20th of a pound). The Everyman's Library continues to this day, but its goal was seized and extended by a much more famous name, Penguin Books.

During the Great Depression publishers struggled to reach a mass market and in 1934, British publishers held a conference at Rippon Hall in Oxford, to discuss how to reach a larger audience. One person in attendance was Allan Lane, who at the time was with Bodley Head, a publishing house founded by his uncle, John Lane. Allan Lane had been managing editor since his uncle's death in 1925 and had already 'crossed swords' with the board of directors over his wish to publish James Joyce's controversial book, "Ulysses".

Allan and his brothers Richard and John devised a plan to publish low-cost pocket books with soft paper covers for sixpence (one-half a shilling). Such cheap books were already available but were associated with the more 'lurid' end of book publishing, while the Lanes' goal was to publish quality literature. The idea was not Lane's own invention. In 1932, in Germany, John Holroyd-Reece, Max Wegner and Kurt Enoch had founded Albatross Books. This company published reprints in a pocket-size format, in a simple, modern font, using paper covers colour-coded by subject (green for travel, orange for fiction, etc.). The Lanes followed the ideas of Albatross exactly, right down to the bird-name title. In fact, although Albatross was closed down by WWII, Kurt Enoch was to go on to become the manager of Penguin USA.

The marketing angle Allan Lane devised came, he claimed, from finding himself on a train platform with nothing to read and thinking of selling books through the then-new invention of vending machines. Lane was clearly quite radical in his views, since he installed the first such machine, dubbed the "Penguincubator", outside a well-known radical and anarchist bookstore on Charing Cross Road called Henderson's.

Other publishers felt that a company founded on the principle of low prices was doomed to failure and shrewdly Lane was able to capitalise on that by buying publication rights to numerous books at low prices, from publishers eager to make some money from such a foolish venture. At first, Penguin was published by Bodley Head, but then Lane sold 63,000 books to Woolworth, the low-price department store. This single sale paid for the

Left: Notice the distinctive Penguin Spines at the top of the pictures, photo taken at Scotney House

Key Facts

- Began in 1935 to publish cheap quality books
- Developed the modern paperback book
- Founded and run by Sir Allan Lane
- Gained notoriety by publishing controversial books such as Lady Chatterley's Lover

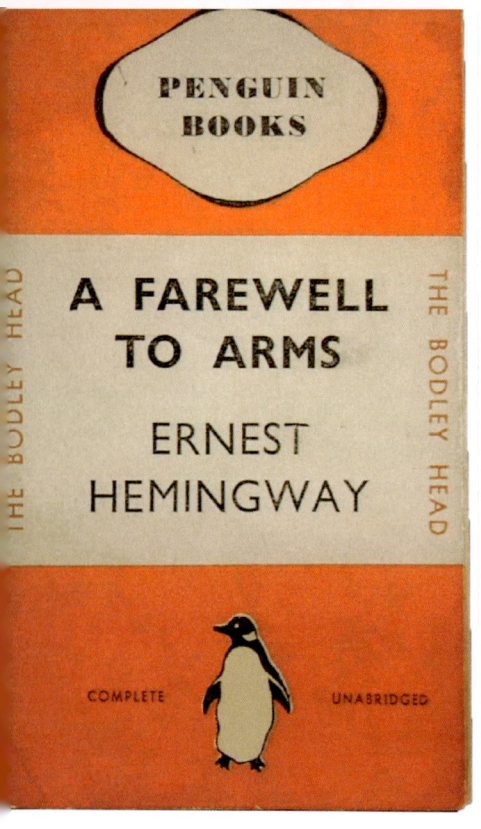  

establishment of Penguin as a separate entity on 30 July 1935. Within a year, Penguin had printed a million books.

The initial design with an upper and lower band of colour, coded by subject, and separated by a band of white, was by Edward Young, a 21-year-old junior office worker, who also drew the first version of the Penguin logo. The company moved to Harmondsworth, west of London, where it remained for the rest of its life as an independent publisher.

The outbreak of WWII proved to be a golden opportunity for Penguin. The demand for cheap books sky-rocketed among both troops and those left at home, and by publishing a range of books related to the war effort, from aircraft recognition guides to how-to guides to keeping poultry at home, Penguin built a solid reputation and image. Lane was also a ruthless businessman and took control of the limited paper supply – paper rationing was in force – through a variety of methods, such as exclusive deals with Canada, paid for in paper and by making an exclusive deal with the British Army to supply all the books for the troops.

When the war ended, paper-rationing did not, and Penguin's access to paper from their wartime deals gave them a significant edge in the post-war market too. In 1946, they sold their 100 millionth book. Lane bought numerous publishing rights from bankrupt publishers at low prices, repeating his early success in doing that, but this time from a position of dominance in the market. In these post-war years, Penguin expanded its series based on topics, with the Penguin Classics series reprinting the kind of classic range pioneered by Everyman. Pelican Books followed, aimed at public education. The first Pelican title was George Bernard Shaw's, The Intelligent Woman's Guide to Socialism and Capitalism. Puffin Books, aimed at the children's market, had started in 1940 and created a completely new market for paperback children's fiction, as well as non-fiction titles.

The traditional literary journals, outlets for new publishing, had died during the war due to paper rationing, and after the war Penguin moved into and dominated, that market with Penguin New Writing, selling 80,000 copies a run. A number of other journals by Penguin only enjoyed brief runs. In 1961 the company went public, and a share-buying frenzy ensued. The share price rose 50% on the first day of trading.

Allan Lane was knighted in 1962, despite having published an unexpurgated version of "Lady Chatterley's Lover" in 1959, to test the Obscene Publications Act of the same year. Penguin won the subsequent trial and dedicated the second edition of the book to the trial jury. In significant contrast, in 1965 Lane stole and burned the entire run of another 'obscene' book, "Massacre" by the French

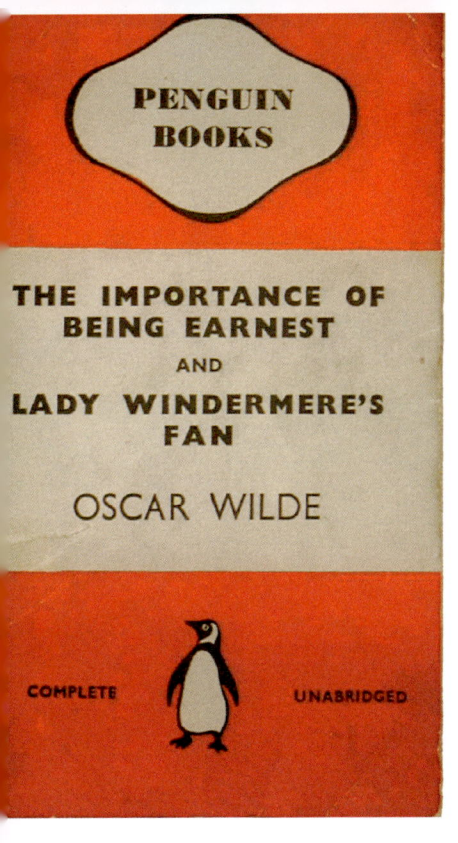

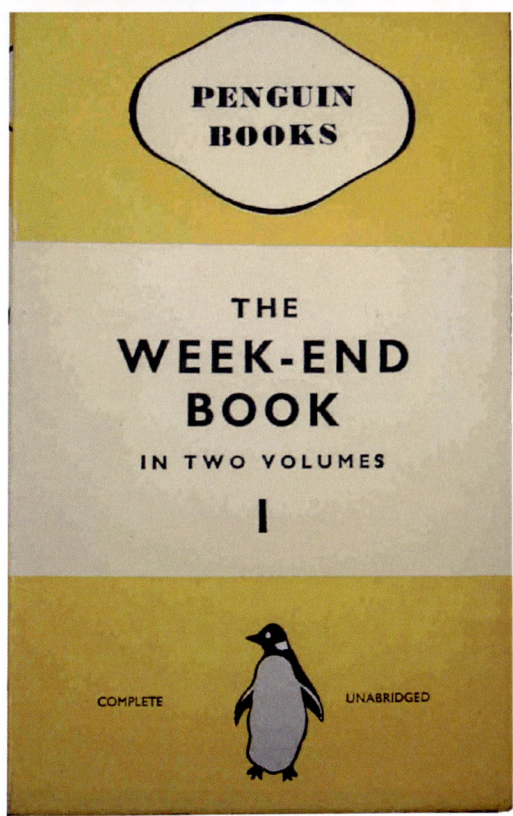

cartoonist Siné, as part of a successful campaign to oust his chief editor, Tony Godwin. Lane retired shortly after and died of cancer in 1970.

Tony Godwin had been influential in modernizing both the company and its graphics, but despite the publicity the company gained from the Lady Chatterley's trial, by the late 60s the company was in financial trouble. A variety of ideas for consortiums with other publishers failed, and six weeks after Lane's death, Penguin was acquired by the educational publisher Pearson PLC. There was a new emphasis on profitability and in the 1990s, Penguin merged with Viking and today is part of the Penguin Random House Group.

Penguin Edition Books of classic literature are still around and you will find a selection of them in most British Bookstores. Many consider them the 'official' version of many works of classic literature as Penguin will collect essays and footnotes that add to the history of the book and enrich the reading experience. They still follow a uniform design aesthetic but they no longer have their distinctive color spines. Occasionally Penguin will release special editions and most recently released a special black edition featuring 80 short excerpts from various works of classic literature. Now, these Penguin shorts have become collector's items in their own right.

Further Research

Several books on the history of the company have been written, including:

Penguin and the Lane Brothers: The Untold Story of a Publishing Revolution, by Stuart Kells (2015). This book is controversial for accusing Allan Lane of mythologizing and exaggerating his own part in the formation and growth of the company.

Penguin by Design: a Cover Story 1935-2005, by Phil Baines, Phil (2007)

The Penguin Story, Harmondsworth, by W. E. Williams (1956)

You can also easily find original Penguin Books from the early days in secondhand bookshops all over Britain.

CHRISTMAS ACTUALLY

From Love Actually to Scrooge - Our Favorite British Holiday Films

By Jonathan Thomas

The Christmas holiday season is our favorite time of year at the Anglotopia offices, and nothing makes the season better than a good British holiday movie. The problem is that there aren't that many - but we've put together our list of favorite British Christmas movies. Some are classics, and some are relatively new but either way, they'll get you in the Christmas spirit.

The Man Who Invented Christmas

At press time, this film hadn't been released yet but judging from the trailers; this is going to become a new holiday favorite. This film, based on a book and starring Dan Stevens (Cousin Matthew from Downton Abbey), this film tells the journey that led to Charles Dickens' creation of "A Christmas Carol," a timeless tale that would redefine the holiday. Many Christmas traditions that we hold dear originated with Dickens, so it will be fun to explore that history in a new historical film. Dan Stevens has done a lot of great work since leaving Downton Abbey so it's exciting to finally see him in a leading role in a new historical drama.

Love Actually

When we surveyed our Anglophile friends and family - this movie was pretty much at the top of everyone's Christmas list. We love this movie too - it's the perfect Christmas movie. The multiple stories, interesting characters and seeing Britain at Christmas make this an enjoyable movie every year. It also provides a fun insight into British Christmas traditions like the annual Christmas party, Christmas pageants and more. We watch this movie at least three times during the holiday season, and it never gets old.

Bridget Jones

The first Bridget Jones movie is framed through Christmas at the beginning and at the end. Bridget may have her foibles but this film undeniably fun and we look forward to watching it every year. This movie introduced Americans to the tradition of the Ugly Christmas Sweater, which has now become a thing over here.

The Muppet Christmas Carol

I grew up with this film, so Michael Caine will always be my Scrooge. While this is not strictly a British movie - it's one of our favorites at Christmastime. It's by far one of our favorite adaptations of A Christmas Carol. The songs are fun, and it's a film we've enjoyed introducing to our own children.

About a Boy

Christmas is tangentially involved in this film and while the subject matter can be quite dark - it's a good movie worth watching. In this film, a cynical, immature young man played by Hugh Grant is taught how to act like a grown-up by a little boy. Hugh's character is a lazy oaf, living off the royalties of a Christmas song that his father wrote that gets played ad nauseam every year. So, Christmas is hovering in the background of this movie at all times (especially when the song starts being played earlier and earlier every year).

The Lion in Winter

Nothing says British Christmas like a historical movie about a King of England spending Christmas at his French chateau played expertly by a classic British cast. It's Christmas 1183, and King Henry II played magnificently by Peter O'Toole, is planning to announce his successor to the throne. The jockeying for the crown, though, is complex. Henry has three sons and wants his boy Prince John to take over. Henry's wife, Queen Eleanor brought to life by Katherine Hepburn, has other ideas. She believes their son Prince Richard should be king. As the family and various schemers gather for the holiday, each tries to make the indecisive king choose their option.

Millions

This movie didn't get a lot of love when it came out - but it's a fun one. The plot imagines a future where Britain is joining the Euro (which seemed possible when it was made, not so much now that they're heading for Brexit!) and what happens when a little boy finds a bag filled with millions of Pounds as the answer to his prayers. This movie was directed by Danny Boyle and features James Nesbitt as the father. It's an uplifting movie about money and hope.

Scrooge - Albert Finney

Really any setting of 'A Christmas Carol' is worth watching but our opinion is that the one with Albert Finney is the best. Released in 1970, this is a musical retelling of Charles Dickens' classic novel about a bitter old miser taken on a journey of self-redemption, courtesy of several mysterious Christmas apparitions.

The Holiday

The Holiday has become a staple in the Anglotopia household since we first saw it a few years ago (despite a huge dislike of the main actress). Two women, played by Kate Winslet and Cameron Diaz, troubled with guy-problems swap homes in each other's countries, where they each meet a local guy and fall in love. Diaz's storyline takes place in a twee little cottage in the English countryside and spends Christmas getting to know Jude Law's suave widower character. It's a little syrupy at times, and the California bits can be trying, but overall, it's a fun film.

A Child's Christmas in Wales

I saw this movie once when I was a kid and recently rediscovered it - it's a great exploration of Christmas during the 'olden times' featuring traditions, songs and more. It's Christmas Eve in Wales. A young boy named Thomas is excited about the holiday, but he's also disappointed because it's raining instead of snowing. His grandfather gives him an old snow globe as an early Christmas present and starts telling colorful, amusing stories about his childhood Christmases that are shown in flashback. Introduced me to the song 'All through the night' a classic Welsh song. It's a wonderful film that's a bit hard to find.

The Holly and the Ivy

This British drama is a cautionary tale about the importance of family, in which parish priest Martin Gregory (Ralph Richardson) has ignored his family to attend to the needs of his parishioners. With his grown children returning for Christmas, including a son on leave from the army, a troubled daughter coming in from London, and a daughter who's sacrificed her own dreams to stay at home with her father, as well as two comic aunts, the emotional tension comes to a head. The film was adapted from a play by Wynyard Browne and eventually sees a happy ending with Martin reconciling with his family.

Arthur Christmas

Aardman arguably represents the best in British animation, and their talents are on full display in this more recent holiday classic. One of many films over the years to tackle how Father Christmas visits all the world's children in one night, this animated feature shows that Christmas is a major operation run by a family of the same name, with Arthur as the younger son of the current Santa Claus. When a child ends up being missed on Christmas Eve, Arthur takes it upon himself to ensure she knows that Santa cares for her too. Several notable Brits lend their voices to the Christmas family, including James McAvoy as Arthur, Hugh Laurie as his brother Edward, Jim Broadbent as Santa, Imelda Staunton as Mrs. Santa, and Bill Nighy as Grandsanta.

Nativity Trilogy

Nearly every child and parent in Britain has had to endure the primary school tradition of the nativity play. In this 2009 film, Martin Freeman plays Paul Maddens, a teacher tasked with stage managing this year's play and saddled with a teaching assistant who may as well be another one of his pupils. To appear greater to a teacher at a rival school, Maddens lies and says that a Hollywood producer is coming to watch their Nativity play. The lie spreads rapidly through the community and hilarity ensues as a result. A sequel was made in 2012 with David Tennant replacing Freeman and a third film released last month sees Martin Clunes as the protagonist.

Bonus: About Time (for New Years)

This film has no parts set at Christmas, but it's a cheeky add to our list because it's become a New Year's tradition for us. The film begins at a New Year's Eve party, so it's the perfect film to ring in your own New Year celebrations. This quirky film by the same director as Love Actually is an underrated film. At the age of 21, Tim (Domhnall Gleeson) discovers he can travel in time and change what happens and has happened in his own life. His decision to make his world a better place by getting a girlfriend turns out not to be as easy as you might think. This movie was marketed as a romance when it was released, which did it a disservice. While the love story is important, the real plot of this movie revolves around the love story between a father and son and coming to terms with the passage of time. Bill Nighy is magnificent as Tim's father.

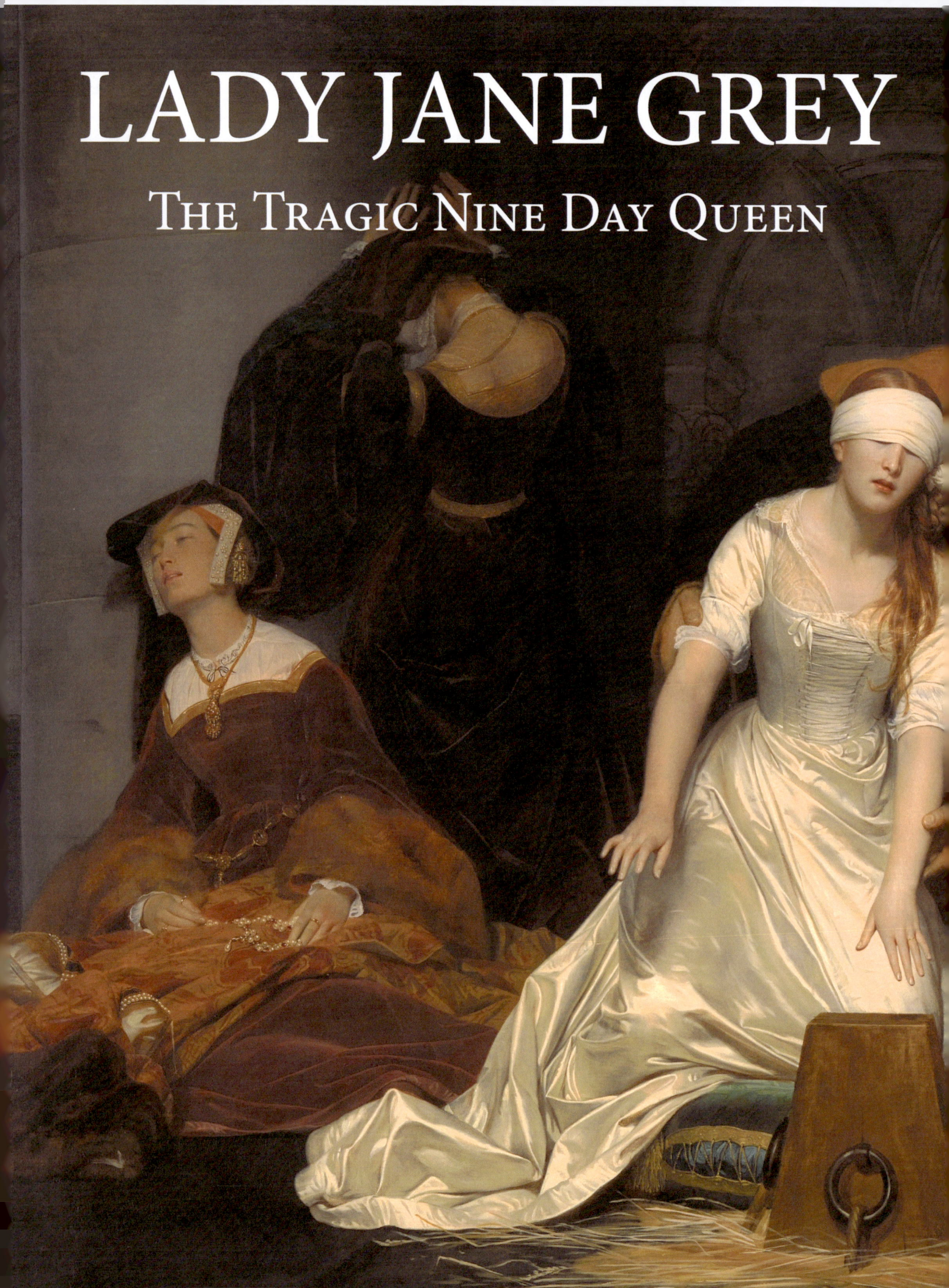

LADY JANE GREY

The Tragic Nine Day Queen

Left: The Execution of Lady Jane Grey, by the French painter Paul Delaroche, 1833

The 'nine-day Queen', Lady Jane Grey is one of the most tragic figures in the history of the monarchy. At just 16 years old the pious and learned young woman had little desire to be proclaimed the Queen of England but through the political machinations of her father the Duke of Suffolk and the powerful Duke of Northumberland, Edward VI's will made it so. Lady Mary Tudor, daughter of Henry VIII and rightful heir did not take this coup lying down and raised enough followers to overthrow Jane in just nine days. Following a stint in the Tower of London, Lady Jane Grey was beheaded aged just sixteen or seventeen years old.

Born in the autumn of 1537, Jane was the daughter of Lady Frances Brandon, the eldest daughter of Mary Tudor, Queen of France, younger sister of Henry VIII, and Henry Grey, the 1st Duke of Suffolk. Through her mother Jane was the great-granddaughter of Henry VII.

In February 1547, aged around 10, Jane joined the household of Thomas Seymour, Edward VI's uncle and Katherine Parr, widow of Henry VIII and queen dowager. Under Katherine's influence Jane received a strict protestant education and grew up to become one of the best-educated young women of her day. Queen Katherine died due to complications related to childbirth soon after Jane joined them and Jane acted as chief mourner at her funeral. In October 1551, King Edward VI made Jane's father, Henry Grey, the Duke of Suffolk and Jane began to appear at the King's Court.

Both Thomas Seymour and Jane's father, Henry Grey used Jane as a pawn to further their own political ambitions and proposed her as a bride for Lord Hertford and the King himself. Neither of these plans came to fruition though and Lady Jane Grey ended up marrying Lord Guildford Dudley, son of John Dudley, 1st Duke of Northumberland and the most powerful man in the country on 25 May 1553 at Durham House.

The Duke of Northumberland acted as regent to King Edward VI and was fiercely protestant. In February 1553, aged just 15, King Edward became terminally ill. At this point Jane was an heiress to the English throne according to her great-uncle King Henry VIII's will but only on the condition that his son Edward and daughters Mary and Elizabeth died without issue.

When it became clear to him that Edward was

Key Facts

- Lady Jane Grey was born in Leicestershire in 1537.
- She was married at the age of 16 to Lord Guildford Dudley, the youngest son of the Duke of Northumberland.
- Lady Jane Grey was secretly proclaimed the Queen of England and Ireland on July 10th 1553 and reigned just nine days before she was seized and imprisoned in the Tower of London
- Jane was executed by beheading on 12 February 1554 aged 16.

dying, the Duke of Northumberland, who already had control of the government, persuaded Edward to sign a will that passed over six feasible claimants to the throne, declared both Mary and Elizabeth Tudor illegitimate and assigned the succession to the Duke of Northumberland's daughter-in-law, Lady Jane Grey.

The Duke and his followers were desperate to stop Mary Tudor, Henry VIII's eldest daughter and Catholic, from taking the throne and when Edward died on 6 July 1553 Jane was informed that she was now queen. Jane took the throne with reluctance and was officially proclaimed Queen of England when she took up residence in the Tower of London. Interestingly Jane refused to name her husband Dudley as king and made him the Duke of Clarence instead.

On hearing of Edward VI's death, Lady Mary Tudor immediately left her residence at Hunsdon foiling the Duke of Northumberland's plot to kidnap her. From a safe place in East Anglia, Mary began to rally her Catholic supporters of which she had many and plan her next move.

As soon as the Duke left London to confront Mary, the privy council saw which way the wind was blowing and switched their allegiance from Jane to Mary, a trend that was adopted even by the Duke of Suffolk, Jane's own father. On 19 July 1553 Mary was proclaimed Queen of England and Jane and her husband were imprisoned in the Tower.

The Duke of Northumberland was executed on 22 August 1553. Jane and her husband were

The Duke of Northumberland

both tried for high treason on 13 November 1553. Both pleaded guilty and were sentenced to death, a sentence that was suspended and might never have been carried out if it wasn't for a rebellion that had nothing at all to do with Jane. On Queen Mary's announcement that she would marry the future Philip II of Spain, a fellow Catholic, those who did not support her joined Sir Thomas Wyatt, The Younger's rebellion, including the Duke of Suffolk, Jane's father. After defeating the rebellion, Queen Mary ordered that Jane and her husband be beheaded along with the Duke of Suffolk.

On 12 February 1554 Guildford was taken to the public execution place at Tower Hill, beheaded, and his corpse taken back to the Tower where Lady Jane was shown his corpse. Lady Jane was then taken to Tower Green where she recited Psalm 51, blindfolded herself and was beheaded. The Duke of Suffolk, Jane's father was executed 11 days later but her mother, the Duchess of Suffolk was given a full pardon, remarried and lived out her days at court with her two surviving daughters.

Legacy

Once seen either as a calculating usurper of the throne or an unwitting political pawn, Lady Jane Grey now has a legacy as the tragic heroine of the reformation. No proven authentic portrait exists of Lady Jane Grey which has allowed popular culture to take every liberty with her appearance and fully realise the image of a beautiful, romantic heroine, destined to be a political and religious martyr. The tale of Lady Jane Grey, who will be 16 or 17 years old forever became legendary thanks in part to The Book of Martyrs by John Foxe which emphasised the young queen's piety and unrelenting faith.

TV and Film

- The Prince and the Pauper (2000) TV
- Lady Jane (1986)
- Elizabeth R (1971) TV series
- Crossed Swords (1977)
- Tudor Rose (1936)
- The Court of Intrigue (1923)

Further Reading

- Plowden, Alison (2011) Lady Jane Grey: Nine Days Queen
- Ives, Eric (2009). Lady Jane Grey: A Tudor Mystery
- de Lisle, Leanda (2009). The Sisters Who Would Be Queen: Mary, Katherine and Lady Jane Grey. A Tudor Tragedy
- Cook, Faith (2005) Nine Day Queen of England: Lady Jane Grey
- Loades, David (1996). John Dudley Duke of Northumberland

Locations to Visit

- The location of Lady Jane Grey's birth is not known but she died at the Tower of London and is buried at St. Peter ad Vincula in London.

HOW TO BRING BRITAIN INTO YOUR CHRISTMAS DINNER

By Jacqueline Thomas

When I think back to the Christmas I spent in England; I am shocked that I actually did it. Not only did we go and spend the holidays in the UK but we made memories of a lifetime. After a dismal holiday season the year before, my husband and I decided to shake things up a bit. We had always wanted to experience Christmas in England, the Christmas in the land of Charles Dickens and tradition.

We packed up our two-year-old son, and six-month-old daughter and flew to England for Christmas. I still cannot believe we traveled during the busiest travel season with two small children and did it relatively well. We spent the first week of our trip in London, where I dabbled in cooking. We stayed in a rented flat with a full kitchen, so I roasted a chicken one night for practice in anticipation of roasting our turkey for Christmas dinner. I love to cook at home, and feel that I am fairly good at it. I have roasted many turkeys over the years for Thanksgiving, and consider myself an accomplished turkey roaster.

However, when it comes to cooking in England, it is a whole different experience. Measurements are different from the American standard. Liquids are measured in metric units; dry goods are measured by weight, and the oven temperature is measured in "gas marks." Logically, I thought it wouldn't be too difficult to simply convert measurements, and in most cases, it wasn't, but it was a massive hassle. Let me just say that Google and I cooked together a lot and I did a lot of rounding up or down to the closest measurement.

British food is very different from American food. Things that are common on our shelves aren't there, so I knew cooking a full Christmas dinner could be tricky. The food there is mostly preservative free, it spoils more quickly and cooks differently. Christmas dinner was surely going to be a learning experience, but I was a fairly decent cook, or so I told myself.

After what had been a very trying week in London, we pulled up to the cottage we rented for Christmas. As we pulled up, we saw the Christmas tree that had been prepared for us lit in the window. It was so beautiful and picturesque that it brought tears to my eyes. We had stayed in the cottage several times, so it felt like we were returning home in a way. I was also relieved to know that I had cooked in the kitchen before and was comfortable

Starters
Selection of British Cheeses and Crackers
Bacon Wrapped Sausages

Mains
Roast Turkey
Mashed Potatoes
Steamed Veg
Yorkshire Puddings

Pudding
Yule Log Cake

cooking there.

Once we settled in, my mind shifted to our Christmas meal. I had brought some family recipes from home to make, but for the most part, I wanted to do my best to create a truly British Christmas dinner. The first thing we sorted out was our turkey. Turkey and Goose are the traditional Christmas birds in Britain for Christmas meals. We had actually ordered it six weeks previously by email. Turkey, while quite inexpensive here in the United States, was pricey in England but we figured that it was a special occasion, so we ordered one. Two days before Christmas the actual turkey farmer delivered it to our door! This certainly felt like something out a Charles Dicken's novel; he even looked the part with his flat cap. We had a small conversation with the farmer who had only butchered the bird the day previously. It turned out that we had driven past the turkey farm on our way into the village, and had seen our dinner out in the field. Talk about fresh and local!

Once our bird was stowed in our fridge, luckily, we had a large fridge, I set to planning the rest of our meal. I made a list and set out to the local grocery store (to do the shopping as the Brits say). I did not have a lot of time to grocery shop, with two small children in tow. I knew my list had to be very detailed because there would be no running out for a forgotten ingredient as everything in the village was closed for Christmas. It was at this point I had wondered if we had made a huge mistake, spending the holiday away from home. Even though I was familiar with Britain, it was different from

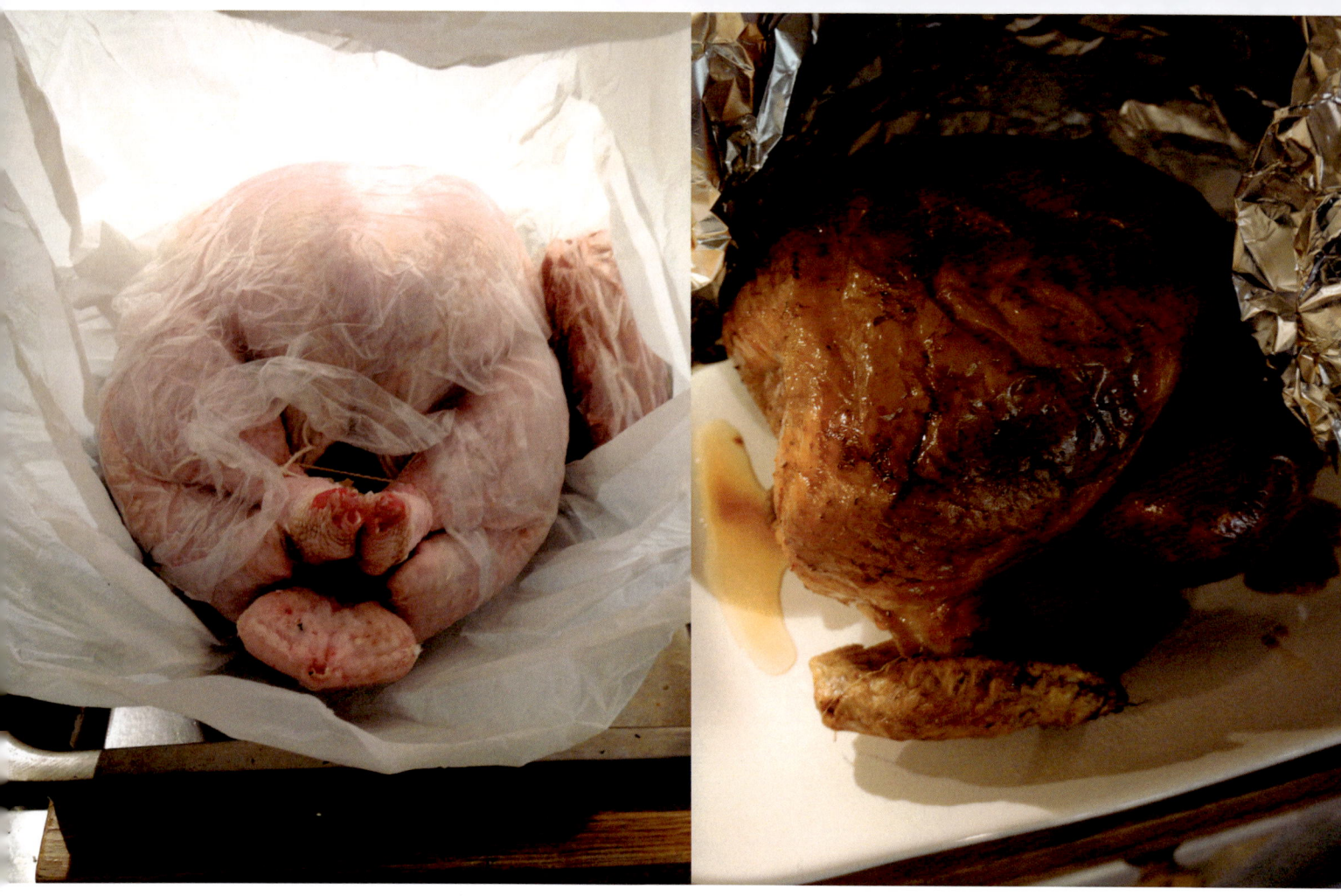

home; even the stores are set up very differently. I practically went to tears over cranberry sauce, not my proudest moment. One simply cannot eat leftover turkey without cranberry sauce. I did end up finding it and everything else my menu required. Our menu looked like this: (see next page)

Christmas morning after the presents were opened, I got dressed and headed into the kitchen to make my first ever British Christmas dinner. I looked up what temperature to roast our turkey at, or which gas mark and got it in the oven right away. The rest of the food was pretty straightforward until I got to the starters. I completely burnt the sausage rolls. My husband didn't say anything, thankfully. It was at this point that I really started to miss my family in the kitchen with me, coming from a large Italian-American family. My poor husband, who recognized that I was a woman on the edge, decided to take the kids out for a walk, and let me have some time to myself to get it together. I opened a bottle of wine, turned on some Christmas music, pulled myself together and cooked on. Most of the meal was pretty much the same as cooking it at home would have been.

Then the point came when it was time to make Yorkshire puddings. I was beyond nervous, but I read the directions carefully and used a British recipe, no conversion necessary. I mixed the batter together and poured it into a small pitcher to rest as I poured oil into the tins and placed them into the oven. The whole process felt very odd, but I told myself to stick to the recipe. Once the oil in the tin was screaming-hot, I pulled it out and quickly poured in the batter and put it right back into the oven. I was delighted when I opened the oven again to see that they actually looked like Yorkshire Puddings!

Overall, the dinner turned out pretty well, but certainly not my best. The turkey turned out a little dry, but we ate it happily in our idyllic little cottage with views of the Blackmore Vale. The meal was bittersweet; we missed our families. We made the best of it and actually had a great time. We pulled our Christmas crackers and wore our paper crowns as we enjoyed our dinner.

The next day, we were invited over to a dear friend's home for a Boxing Day lunch. It was our first Boxing day lunch ever. This was the first time I was introduced to pork pies and pickle. At home, pies with meat in them are rare and are usually served hot with gravy inside. I nervously tried a slice of the cold meat pie as we sat down to dinner when I noticed a jar being passed around the table with what looked like some sort of chutney inside. Our friends introduced me to pickle. It's not actually pickles but a variety of diced pickled vegetable in a vinegar apple and tomato sauce. I was instantly smitten! We also had a lovely selection of cheeses. My friend's Boxing Day lunch was much tastier than my Christmas dinner had been. That night before we left for our cottage, they gave me a jar of pickle to take with me. A few hours later, slightly hungry, I went and pulled out some cold turkey and put a heaping spoonful of pickle on my plate. I also heated up some macaroni and cheese to go with. I sent a picture of my little meal to my friends who felt that my combination of foods was certainly interesting. I guess some things are lost in translation.

Looking back, I smile at my inexperience, but I learned some very valuable lessons about cooking in Britain. First and most important, when cooking in Britain, use a British recipe or know your own recipe well enough to not have to measure. Ironically, we picked up some food traditions from that Christmas, none of which I cooked. We had our first mince pies and were instantly smitten, as well as mulled wine, not to mention pork pies and pickle.

Last Christmas, I thought to myself at home in the States, what I would give for a homemade mince pie and a glass of mulled wine. After trying the pre-packaged mince pies, which were yummy but not the real thing, I decided to make my own. A year ago, the owner of the cottage we stayed in and a dear friend, Jane, published her family's mince pie recipe in our holiday issue of the magazine. I had purchased the necessary equipment to cook British recipes in my own kitchen after learning that some recipes simply didn't turn out well if they were converted. I set off to my local grocery store in search of the ingredients and found it amusing that I couldn't find some of the ingredients. It felt like the cranberry sauce, incident all over again, minus the meltdown. Luckily, I have become a better cook and was able to swap out a few substations. The first ingredient that I could not find anywhere was sultanas. I think they are a cross between a dried cranberry and a raisin. No one had them. I could not find mixed peel, some of the sugars, or the suet. I managed substitute what I needed by adding dried figs, black and golden raisins, fruit cake mixture

Starters
Bacon wrapped Sausages
Bacon wrapped figs (Devils on Horseback)
Selection of British Cheeses and Crackers
Fresh Shrimp
Seasonally Spiced Nuts

Mains
Beef Standing Rib Roast with Port and Stilton Gravy
Mashed Potatoes
Red Cabbage with Pomegranate Juice
Yorkshire Puddings
Roasted Brussel Sprouts
Cranberry Sauce

Pudding
Mice Pies
Mulled Wine
Panettone Bread Pudding

(similar to mixed peel) which I pulled the candied cherries out of and vegetable lard in place of the suet. I was also able to find some of the sugars at my local health food store. I could've placed an order for all of the items from Amazon, but this time I found hunting for the ingredients to be a lot of fun.

Once I collected all of my ingredients I could not wait to get started. I conferred with my Jane who found some of my substitutions to be interesting. The day came, and I set a large pot of wine to mull on the cooktop while I baked. Luckily, Jane had told me that in order to make the crust truly irresistible to make it by hand. I had not made the dough by hand in quite a while, but I learned after watching many episodes of the Great British Bake Off to do as the recipe says when it comes to pastry. I measured out all of my ingredients on my scale and set to putting the dough together by hand. I looked Longingly at my Kitchen Aid as I used just my fingertips to lift and incorporate the mixture together. By the end, my hands ached, and I have strong hands as a knitter. I put the dough in the fridge to rest as the directions stated and helped myself to a glass of mulled wine.

I moved onto making my Anglo-American mince pie filling as I sipped my wine. I chopped

Yorkshire Puddings

all of my ingredients finely and added a dash of whiskey to my mixture. It took everything in me not to eat the mince with a spoon. My kitchen smelled of cinnamon, cloves, and dried fruits. Once the mince had come together, I pulled out the dough and rolled it out. I am so glad I listened to Jane's instructions, the pastry dough was so luxurious to work with, by far the best pastry dough I have ever made!

I once again had to substitute some kitchen equipment, I didn't have the round cutter in the size that was recommended, so I used the top ring of a Mason jar lid, which worked pretty well. I also had to use a small cupcake tin to cook the pies in since I did not have a tart pan. I cut out about 20 bottoms and placed them gently in the pan. Then I filled my pies with a hearty spoonful of the mince. I rolled out and cut the tops and topped each of the pies. Luckily, I remembered, again from many episodes of The Great British Bake Off, to seal my pies, no one likes a leaky pie, no matter how delicious the filling is.

I nervously put them in the oven, as I prayed they'd turn out. I helped myself to another glass of mulled wine, to calm my baking jitters. After about five minutes, the smell of the baking pies permeated my house, and I soon had a crowd in the kitchen. As my timer went off, I nervously pulled my pies out of the oven. They looked beautiful, and not leaky, so far it was a success. Now the real nerve-wracking moment came, as I had swapped a tart pan for a cupcake pan, I had to turn the pan over to get the pies out. The cupcake spots were deep in my pan so I could not pry them out without cracking the delicate crust. I nervously turned them out after a minute of rest. I heard all six pies tumble out. They were baked beautifully, I was absolutely thrilled, as I imagined Paul Hollywood saying, "these have a good bake." but probably not worthy of a coveted handshake. I set them on a tray to cool, but not before I tasted one, then tasted another and so on. They were delicious! Excitedly, I sent my Jane a picture of the finished pies, and they met her approval. I ended up making several batches of mince pies last season; everyone loved them.

That little taste of Britain set us off on wanting a true British Christmas dinner once again. I felt that since the pies had been such a success that I could conquer dinner this time. Instead of turkey, we ordered a beef standing rib roast. I had found

a Nigella Lawson Christmas cookbook, Nigella Christmas, at a bookstore earlier in the year and used it as a primer. Our menu was as follows: (see previous page)

This time my British dinner turned out much better than my first attempt. I didn't burn anything! I was a little nervous to serve my British themed Christmas dinner since my family seems to prefer more traditional American Christmas fair. It was a huge hit. It was the first time that Brussel sprouts and red cabbage had ever sat on my Christmas table. They will now always sit on my Christmas table, along with most of this menu. This meal tasted more British than the dinner I had actually made in Britain.

Cooking a British recipe in an American kitchen can really be tricky, and vice versa. I feel that if my Christmas kitchen had a geographic location, it would be found somewhere in the middle of the Atlantic Ocean. I've found that trying to "translate" recipes to either content is very tricky so; I simply don't do it. I have bought the necessary equipment for my kitchen to cook British recipes. I also highly recommend Nigella Lawson's Nigella Christmas cookbook. The recipes have been converted for an American audience. I look forward to my British-American cooking skills growing further, as we yearn for a taste of our second home on our Christmas table.

A BRIEF HISTORY OF HOVIS BREAD

The Bread That Made This The Most Famous Hill in Britain

By Jonathan Thomas

Long before there were whole-foods and artisan bakers, there was Hovis. This loaf of 'brown bread' had been on almost every British table for more than 100 years, and it is still going strong. Many English people have fond memories of tiny 'penny' loaves of Hovis as their daily bread. The loaf and its special flour, enriched with wheat-germ, was invented in the north of England in the 1880s, by a village miller Richard 'Stoney' Smith. His bread quickly spread across the country by clever marketing and an early kind of franchise operation using local bakers. So important did it become that the government took it over as an emergency measure during WWII. The company always promoted the health benefits of its bread, even before the vitamin content of wheat-germ was discovered. A Hovis TV ad from the 1970s was voted 'Best TV Ad Ever' in a poll in 2006. The company is today a large corporation, but the 'home-baked' image endures for this loaf in the minds of most British people.

We tend to think of healthy eating as something modern, but most food historians agree that in the 19th-century people ate healthily. They may have consumed lots of carbohydrates, and fats, but they also ate lots of vegetables too. With all their physical activity they needed that bread and potatoes for energy, but white bread, with all the bran and wheat-germ removed, was the standard. This was because flour with the wheat germ in it went rancid quickly, as the oils in the germ decomposed, so it did not store or travel well. For feeding people in the growing cities of the Industrial Revolution, without refrigeration or cooling available, it had to be removed shortly after the flour was ground. The germ and bran removed were used chiefly as cattle food.

People knew little about vitamins at that time, but they did know that the germ of the wheat was nutritious, and people's diet would be improved if they ate it. It was up to a miller in a remote part of Britain to come up with the solution. Richard 'Stoney' Smith, was born on 16 February 1836, in the mill house opposite the water-powered mill in the small town of Stone, Staffordshire. There had been a mill on the site since the Middle Ages, but the one Stoney's father ran had been built by a certain Robert Bill in 1795. It had two large millstones and could produce 180 pounds of flour an hour, and was driven by water cascading down the mill-race onto a 25-foot diameter water-wheel.

KEY FACTS

- Patented in 1887 by Richard 'Stoney' Smith, a village miller.
- Uses steaming to make it possible to retain the wheat-germ in flour
- Became a standard item on the table for its claims of health benefits
- Occupies a special place as a symbol of home goodness

Smith's idea was to lightly steam the wheatgerm, and so stabilise it and prevent it going bad. Then he put it back into the flour, and he realised he could put back as much as he wanted – which he did. His flour had three times more germ than natural flour. He patented the process in 1887, in both the UK and the USA, and dubbed it 'Smith's Patent Germ Flour'. From this he baked bread, and call that, 'Smith's Patent Germ Bread'. The same year he joined a much larger milling and baking firm, S. Fitton & Sons Ltd, in the town of Macclesfield, Cheshire. He was given a seat on the board, probably in return for his valuable patents, and he was to die in 1900.

The new bread could not have come at a better time, as there was a surge in interest in healthy eating, perhaps in part because of the unnatural and unsanitary crowding in the rapidly-expanding cities. The problem was in the name, which was anything but appealing, or even remotely exciting. So Fitton & Sons organised a competition, offering £25 for a name for their loaf. The name 'Yum Yum' did not win, but it did come second. The winning entry was by an Oxford schoolteacher with the Dickensian name of Herbert Grime. Mr Grime showed his erudite Latin skills by shortening the phrase, 'hominis vis', meaning 'the strength of man', into the crisper 'Hovis'. The word Hovis was registered as a Trade Mark in 1890. A few years later, across the Atlantic, Will Smith Kellogg released his Corn Flakes in 1906, similarly marketed as a health food.

Thomas Fitton was the driving force of the firm at that time, and with its new name, and now necessary for all growing children, according to the advertisements of the day, Hovis became a big

hit. The company also claimed at the time that 1½ pounds of this bread was more nutritious than 1 pound of white bread and ½ pound of beef steak (and much more digestible). Since it was also Supplied to the Queen and Royal Family and a Cure for Indigestion, its success was assured. Fitton & Sons sold the flour to local bakers, who baked it in tins that stamped the name right into the loaf. By this distribution and franchise method, they were already selling a million loaves a week by 1898. To help supply the bakers of London they had, in 1896, purchased Imperial Mills, on the Embankment, right in central London along the River Thames. In 1898 Fitton & Sons changed their name to 'The Hovis Bread Flour Company'.

Part of the new healthy society was the craze for cycling, and in a remarkable presaging of the Google Maps strategy, Hovis brought out their 'Cycle Road Maps and Guides' that not only contained advertising for the bread, but indicated on the map tea-shops where it could be bought as part of the great British institution, high tea.

In 1918, 'Hovis Limited' was launched as a public company. In 1920, expanded on their success with cycle maps, Hovis published 'Where to Go and How to Get There: Hovis Road Map of England, Wales, and Scotland'. With the discovery of B vitamins in wheatgerm in 1924 sales received a further boost. With competition from other 'brown bread' manufacturers growing, they developed the slogan Don't Just Say Brown – Say Hovis, which was first seen in 1924. Following the entry into the company of Cecil Gordon Wood in 1928, a period of expansion began, and Hovis acquired mills in England and overseas. By the beginning of the 1930s they had 20,000 bakers producing their bread every day, and proudly displaying a gold 'Hovis' sign on their store fronts. The bread came in a both a one-pound and a two-pound loaf, as well as an 8-ounce 'junior' loaf and 'mini' loaves that sold for one penny and were loved by children.

In 1940, their mill in Manchester was destroyed by German bombs. The government took control of the company as an emergency war measure. Marketing slogans became exhortations to economy with Thin Slices Make Hovis Go Further, and Make Hovis Your Ration. They also introduced a granary loaf, with cracked wheat in the mixture.

Following the war, the company continued to grow, and in 1957 it merged with the flour business

McDougall. Shortly afterward, in 1962, the new company added another flour-miller, Joseph Rank, and become Rank Hovis McDougall.

For their advertising Hovis had always used the best. In the 1930s, they hired Heath Robinson, a cartoonist of eccentric and impossible machines, as an illustrator. Mabel Lucie Atwell, famous for the coy and nostalgic illustrations of little girls, was also hired. So too was Tom Eckersley, whose stylish, modern work could not have been further away from either Robinson or Atwell. The high point in their numerous campaigns was the TV advertisement created by the British film director Ridley Scott. Scott had not yet become famous for the film Alien. He filmed a boy pushing a bicycle, carrying a large basket filled with loaves of Hovis, up Gold Hill, in the market town of Shaftesbury, Dorset. Dvorak's New World Symphony plays in the background. The hill, a quintessentially British cobble lane lined with charming houses, was the perfect setting to evoke the nostalgia of hand-baked loaves from the village baker, even if Hovis was by then a giant multinational. The ad was voted the UK's all-time favourite commercial in 2006.

Shaftesbury has now become one of the most famous towns in England, with people coming from all over the world to visit the hill. Many people thought it was in the North of England because Hovis is a northern company and the hills looked vaguely like Yorkshire. People are always surprised to find out it's located in Northern Dorset.

It's also not a quaint little village but a thriving market down. Gold Hill is just one of many streets in the town of 7,000+ people. It's located directly behind the Town Hall, and you will find tourists taking pictures pretty much any time of the year, it's a popular top for pensioners. There's a lovely cafe at the top of the hill where you can get a cup of tea and cake while you watch the views over the Blackmore Vale.

There are many fantastic walks in and around Shaftesbury and if you intend to stay a few days, pop into the Shaftesbury Tourist Information Centre where they can provide you with tons of great things to see and do locally. The Hovis ad lives in a particular part of the British consciousness and sense of self, harking back to a simpler time. While those times are long gone, they are not forgotten when it comes to memories like this.

A consequence of the street's fame is that there

are lots of tourists visiting but also lots of major events that take place on the hill as well. Most notable is the Gold Hill Cheese run where locals compete to carry the biggest roll of cheese up the hill; this usually takes place during the yearly Shaftesbury Food & Drink Festival. The real estate on the hill is also extremely valuable due to the fame of the scene - houses on Gold Hill can cost $750,000 or more depending on how large they are (and there's nowhere to park except at the bottom of the hill.

Since the famous Gold Hill ad, the company has diversified its range of loaves, and today it is 51% owned by the global equity firm The Gores Group, headquartered in Los Angeles. The remaining 49% is held by Premier Foods, who also own several other iconic British food-brands, including Mr Kipling, Sharwood's, and Oxo. A Very British Brand has become less British over the years, but their heritage is still beloved - as are their products. Pick up a loaf on your next trip - it makes the BEST toast.

Sites to Visit

Hovis loaves, in both the traditional format and newer, innovative versions, can be bought in every British grocery store sizes. It is still a standard item on many household tables.

Gold Hill is a popular destination in the town of Shaftesbury, Dorset. There is a large replica Hovis loaf, with a collection slot for local charities, at the top of the hill.

Richard Smith is buried in Highgate Cemetery, North London.

THE SLANG PAGE
Scottish English

Here is a list of common Scottish English words and phrases. This is not meant to be an exhaustive list but an overview of the most commonly used phrases. Generally, words that are used commonly throughout the rest of Britain have been excluded from the list.

Auld - Old.
Arse / erse - Bum.
Aye - Yes.
Bairn - A baby.
Brassic - Skint.
Braw - Beautiful.
Breek - Trousers.
Cannae - Can not.
Doon - Down.
Dreich - Cold as in it's a driech day outside. Dug - A dog.
Feert - To be scared, afeared (I'm feert of the dark).
Glasgow Kiss - A headbutt. Glesga - Glasgow.
Dafty - Silly.
Dinnae - Don't ("Dinnae dae that!").
Dobber - A fool/stupid person. Also means "dickhead" ("Whit ye daein ya dobber?!").
Jaked - Being in a state of drunkenness (I was jaked last night).
Lang - Surname.
Lecky - Electricity - often used in reference to bills (she didn't pay her lecky this month).
Loch - Lake.
I dinnae ken - Don't know.
Mibay - Maybe.
Minted - Rich/wealthy ("Look at his motor, he must be minted.).
Nae danger - No problem ("Ye want mince and totties fur yur dinner? Nae danger").
Napper - Head.

Naw - No.
Nip - Kiss a single measure of an alcoholic spirit, often whisky.
Nippin - Stinging.
Numpty - A useless individual/ moron.
Nut - 1. Head 2. Or another term used for the word no.
Oaf - Off.
Oan yer bike - Go away.
Oan yer trolley - Go away.
Oot - Out.
Outwith - Outside.
Pan - Break or disfigure ("pan the windows in").
Peely wally - Pale or pasty. Pish - Piss.
Pure - Very, totally ("she's pure no right".) used to emphasis something.
Quality - Great/excellent ("That film was quality.").
Radge - A fit of rage.
Roamin - Taking a walk.
Scheme - Residential area usually council estate.
Scunner - One who pisses you off.
Scunnered - To be pissed off.
Shite - Shit.
Skiddies - Gentleman's undergarments with traces of last nights dinner.
Skuddy - Naked.
Talking oot yer fanny flaps - Lying. Very rude.
Tan - Smash windows (I'm gonny tan yer windaes).
Tanned - To drink/drunk or to vandalise.
Tatties/tatters - Potatoes.
That's a sin - What a shame.
Toaty - Small/tiny.
Tube - An idiot/fool. Twally - A person of lesser intellect.
Waldies - Wellies.
Wee – Little/small.
Wee small - A child.

www.ingramcontent.com/pod-product-compliance
Lightning Source LLC
Chambersburg PA
CBRC090017090526
44589CB00008BA/81